高等院校互联网+新形态教材·经管系列(二维码版)

商务英语函电
(微课版)

赵凤玉　黄兴运　李一枝　主　编
谢有琪　蒋　霞　刘　敏　李秀进　副主编

清华大学出版社
北京

内 容 简 介

随着全球贸易的蓬勃发展与国际商务活动的日渐频繁，商务信函写作愈显其重要性，本书正是基于此背景编撰。全书共 11 个单元，包含商务英语函电写作基础知识及外贸业务流程信函写作，主要涵盖建立贸易关系、询盘、发盘、还盘、订单及确认、包装、支付、运输、保险、索赔及理赔等贸易磋商过程的真实案例、专业背景知识、写作技巧、函件样信、主要词汇及句型、练习等。

本书是中国大学 MOOC 平台 SPOC 课程《商务英语函电》配套教材，配有系列教学视频、PPT 课件、练习参考答案等，内容按"案例分析→专业背景知识→函电写作技巧→样信分析→重点术语、词汇、句型汇总→课后练习"的顺序编排，具有鲜明的综合性、应用性、实践性与跨学科性的专业化与职业化特征。

本教材适合商务英语、国际贸易、跨境电子商务等专业，以及英语专业商务、经贸方向本、专科学生使用，也可供外经贸从业者及相关工作人员使用。

本书封面贴有清华大学出版社防伪标签，无标签者不得销售。
版权所有，侵权必究。举报：010-62782989，beiqinquan@tup.tsinghua.edu.cn。

图书在版编目(CIP)数据

商务英语函电：微课版 / 赵凤玉, 黄兴运, 李一枝 主编. -- 北京：清华大学出版社, 2024. 10. -- (高等院校互联网+新形态教材). -- ISBN 978-7-302-67235-7
Ⅰ.F740
中国国家版本馆 CIP 数据核字第 20242J5F23 号

责任编辑：梁媛媛
装帧设计：李 坤
责任校对：常 婷
责任印制：刘海龙

出版发行：清华大学出版社
网　　址：https://www.tup.com.cn, https://www.wqxuetang.com
地　　址：北京清华大学学研大厦 A 座　　邮　编：100084
社 总 机：010-83470000　　邮　购：010-62786544
投稿与读者服务：010-62776969, c-service@tup.tsinghua.edu.cn
质量反馈：010-62772015, zhiliang@tup.tsinghua.edu.cn
课件下载：https://www.tup.com.cn, 010-62791865

印 装 者：三河市人民印务有限公司
经　　销：全国新华书店
开　　本：185mm×260mm　　印 张：12.75　　字 数：310 千字
版　　次：2024 年 9 月第 1 版　　印 次：2024 年 9 月第 1 次印刷
定　　价：46.00 元

产品编号：103573-01

前言

本书以商务英语、国际贸易、电子商务类等专业本科教学质量国家标准及国家有关高等教育改革的相关文件精神为理论依据，以不断深化高等学校本科教育教学改革，创新人才培养模式，提高专业人才培养质量为实践依据，旨在突出商务英语语言运用、商务英语知识与实践、跨文化商务交际能力的培养目标，具有综合性、应用性、实践性与跨学科性的专业化与职业化特征，适合高等院校商务英语、国际贸易、国际市场营销、跨境电子商务等专业，以及英语专业商务、经贸方向本、专科学生使用。

全书共 11 个单元，包含商务英语函电写作基础知识与外贸业务流程信函写作两部分。核心内容涵盖建立贸易关系、询盘、发盘、还盘、订单及确认、包装、支付、运输、保险、索赔及理赔等贸易磋商过程的函件内容。全书核心内容外贸业务流程信函写作部分按"案例分析→专业背景知识→商务英语函电写作原则→样信分析→重点术语、词汇、句型汇总→课后练习"的顺序编排，便于教师采用案例教学、项目教学、模块教学与模拟教学等方法，增强易学性，从而激发学生学习兴趣和潜能。本书配有专业词汇、常用句式和习惯表达的实例，并针对不同技能和知识目标，设计了术语、句子、信件翻译题、选择题、填空题、写作题等，以训练学习者的商务知识、语言知识、写作能力等，实现边学边用、学以致用的职业能力目标。

此外，本书还配有 60 个教学视频、各类练习及讨论话题，融合国际经贸基本知识、商务函电写作、国际商务礼仪及跨文化交际等知识与技能，配套资源丰富多样。本书将跨文化商务英语写作能力与外贸业务能力紧密结合，可以灵活地采用案例导入，引导学生发现问题，便于教师在教学中实现由易及难、由浅入深、循序渐进的讲解。本书涵盖商务英语函电涉及的经济贸易基本概念、理论知识、英语语言运用以及函电写作方法技巧，使相对枯燥和程式化的商务英语专业写作理论知识变得生动易懂，以激发学生的学习兴趣和潜能。

本书由南宁师范大学赵凤玉、广西师范大学黄兴运、桂林航天工业学院李一枝任主编，桂林航天工业学院谢有琪、桂林理工大学蒋霞、广西体育高等专科学校刘敏、广西城市职业大学李秀进任副主编。其中，赵凤玉、黄兴运、李一枝负责编写第 1 至第 10 单元的课文和练习，以及全书的汇编、校对等工作，谢有琪负责编写第 3 至第 5 单元的练习及参与全书的汇编工作，蒋霞负责编写第 11 单元的课文及练习，刘敏、李秀进负责汇编全书课后词汇、句型及参与全书的汇编工作。

本教材由"南宁师范大学教材建设基金"资助出版，在此深表谢意。同时，本教材也是 2024 年度广西高等教育本科教学改革工程项目(项目编号：2024JGB265)及广西教育科学"十四五"规划 2023 年度"三进"工作外语教学改革研究专项课题(项目编号：2023ZJY2359)的阶段性成果。

由于编者水平有限，书中疏漏之处在所难免，敬请广大读者批评指正。

编 者

目录

Unit 1　Structure and Layout of Business English Correspondence 1

1.1　Introduction 1
1.2　The Structure of Business Letters 2
　　1.2.1　The Seven Principle Parts 2
　　1.2.2　The Optional Parts 6
1.3　The Layout of Business Letters 9
　　1.3.1　The Styles of Business Letters 9
　　1.3.2　Envelopes Addressing 14
Useful Words & Expressions 16
Exercises 17

Unit 2　Writing Principles 21

2.1　Introduction 21
2.2　The Principles of Business Letter Writing 22
　　2.2.1　The Principle of Consideration 22
　　2.2.2　The Principle of Courtesy 24
　　2.2.3　The Principle of Conciseness 26
　　2.2.4　The Principle of Clarity 28
　　2.2.5　The Principle of Concreteness 30
　　2.2.6　The Principle of Correctness 31
　　2.2.7　The Principle of Completeness 31
Useful Words & Expressions 32
Exercises 33

Unit 3　Establishing Business Relations 35

3.1　Background Knowledge 35
　　3.1.1　Case Study 35
　　3.1.2　Relevant Information 36
　　3.1.3　Writing Skills 37
3.2　Sample Letters and Basic Writing Structure Analysis 38
　　3.2.1　Basic Writing Structures of Seeking New Clients Letters 38
　　3.2.2　Basic Writing Structures of Letters About Establishing Business Relations 39

3.2.3 Basic Writing Structures of Letters About Credit Inquiry 40

 Useful Words & Expressions 44

 Exercises 48

Unit 4 Inquiries and Replies 53

 4.1 Background Knowledge 53

  4.1.1 Case Study 53

  4.1.2 Relevant Information 54

  4.1.3 Writing Skills 55

 4.2 Sample Letters and Basic Writing Structure Analysis 56

  4.2.1 Basic Writing Structures of Inquiry Letters 56

  4.2.2 Basic Writing Structures of Favorable Replies to Inquiry Letters ... 58

  4.2.3 Basic Writing Structures of Unfavorable Replies to Inquiry Letters ... 60

 Useful Words & Expressions 62

 Exercises 66

Unit 5 Offers and Counter-offers 71

 5.1 Background Knowledge 71

  5.1.1 Case Study 71

  5.1.2 Relevant Information 72

  5.1.3 Writing Skills 73

 5.2 Sample Letters and Basic Writing Structure Analysis 74

  5.2.1 Basic Writing Structures of Offer Letters 74

  5.2.2 Basic Writing Structures of Counter-offer Letters 76

  5.2.3 Basic Writing Structures of Replies to Counter-offer Letters 78

 Useful Words & Expressions 79

 Exercises 81

Unit 6 Orders and Acknowledgements 85

 6.1 Background Knowledge 85

  6.1.1 Case Study 85

  6.1.2 Relevant Information 86

  6.1.3 Writing Skills 87

 6.2 Sample Letters and Basic Writing Structure Analysis 88

  6.2.1 Basic Writing Structures of Order Letters 88

  6.2.2 Basic Writing Structures of Replies to Order Letters 90

 Useful Words & Expressions 93

 Exercises 96

Unit 7 Packing 101

- 7.1 Background Knowledge 101
  - 7.1.1 Case Study 101
  - 7.1.2 Relevant Information 102
  - 7.1.3 Writing Skills 104
- 7.2 Sample Letters and Basic Writing Structure Analysis 105
  - 7.2.1 Basic Writing Structures of Letters Concerning Packing Proposal 105
  - 7.2.2 Basic Writing Structures of Letters Concerning Packing Instructions 106
  - 7.2.3 Basic Writing Structures of Letters Informing the Details of Packing 107
  - 7.2.4 Basic Writing Structures of Letters for Improving Future Packing 108
- Useful Words & Expressions 110
- Exercises 114

Unit 8 Payment 119

- 8.1 Background Knowledge 119
  - 8.1.1 Case Study 119
  - 8.1.2 Relevant Information 120
  - 8.1.3 Writing Skills 122
- 8.2 Sample Letters and Basic Writing Structure Analysis 124
  - 8.2.1 Basic Writing Structures of Letters Concerning Terms of Payment Proposal 124
  - 8.2.2 Basic Writing Structures of Letters Urging Establishment of L/C 126
  - 8.2.3 Basic Writing Structures of Letters Notifying the Establishment of L/C 127
  - 8.2.4 Basic Writing Structures of L/C Amendment Letters 128
- Useful Words & Expressions 129
- Exercises 133

Unit 9 Shipment 139

- 9.1 Background Knowledge 139
  - 9.1.1 Case Study 139
  - 9.1.2 Relevant Information 140
  - 9.1.3 Writing Skills 141
- 9.2 Sample Letters and Basic Writing Structure Analysis 143
  - 9.2.1 Basic Writing Structures of Letters Concerning Sending Shipping Instructions 143
  - 9.2.2 Basic Writing Structures of Letters Concerning Urging an Early Shipment 144
  - 9.2.3 Basic Writing Structures of Reply Letters to Urging an Early Shipment 145
  - 9.2.4 Basic Writing Structures of Letters Concerning Shipping Advice 147
- Useful Words & Expressions 149

Exercises 154

Unit 10 Insurance 159

  10.1 Background Knowledge 159

    10.1.1 Case Study 159

    10.1.2 Relevant Information 160

    10.1.3 Writing Skills 162

  10.2 Sample Letters and Basic Writing Structure Analysis 163

    10.2.1 Basic Writing Structures of Letters Concerning the Coverage 163

    10.2.2 Basic Writing Structures of Letters Concerning Excessive Insurance Coverage 164

    10.2.3 Basic Writing Structures of Letters Concerning Asking the Seller to Cover Insurance 165

    10.2.4 Basic Writing Structures of Letters Concerning Insurance Clause 167

  Useful Words & Expressions 169

  Exercises 173

Unit 11 Complaints and Adjustments 179

  11.1 Background Knowledge 179

    11.1.1 Case Study 179

    11.1.2 Relevant Information 180

    11.1.3 Writing Skills 181

  11.2 Sample Letters and Basic Writing Structure Analysis 182

    11.2.1 Basic Writing Structures of Letters Concerning Complaints or Claims 182

    11.2.2 Basic Writing Structures of Letters Concerning Dealing with Complaints or Claims 184

  Useful Words & Expressions 185

  Exercises 190

Bibliography 195

Unit 1 Structure and Layout of Business English Correspondence

1.1 Introduction

Business English correspondence refers to the letters, cables, telexes, faxes and e-mails used in exchanging information in international business, sometimes also in domestic trade. With the rapid development of Internet technology, at present most business communication is carried out on the phone, through social media, or by means of fax or e-mail instead of traditional post, but business correspondence is still of vital importance in international trade. Proper business letters help a company to communicate more efficiently and bring business opportunities to the company. Moreover, letters are the bases of other writing styles as their structure, format, vocabulary, writing skills, etc. are derived from letters. Therefore, the writing of business letters is one of the essential skills for every businessman to bear.

Although the formality in business letter writing is rapidly giving way to a less conventional and friendlier style, the layout still follows a more or less set pattern determined by custom. It is recommended to follow the established practice so as to avoid confusion and a waste of time for both the sender and the receiver.

However, to write business English correspondence well is not that easy. One has to be familiar with the relevant business process and has the knowledge of the basic rules and international trade conventions. The first step is to be acquainted with the layout and basic parts of a business letter.

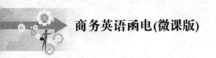

1.2 The Structure of Business Letters

Generally speaking, a fully-constructed business letter is made up of seven principle parts. Except these, there are six optional parts, sometimes applicable accordingly. All the parts are listed in details below with examples to illustrate them.

1.2.1 The Seven Principle Parts

The seven principle parts in a formal business letter are as follows:

- Letterhead
- Date
- Inside Name & Address
- Salutation
- Body
- Complimentary Close
- Signature

1. The Letterhead

The letterhead expresses a firm's personality and forms one's impression of the writer's firm. The styles vary greatly but all give similar information, including company name, address, postal code, telephone numbers, fax numbers, e-mail address, website, logo (sometimes, if any) and sometimes maybe the kind of business the firm handles. It is usually printed in the up-center or at the left margin of a letter. Please refer to the following examples:

> Nanning ASEAN Fruit Trading Co., Ltd.
> 100 Youyi Road
> Qingxiu District
> Nanning 530022, P. R. China
> Tel: 0086-771-21899899
> Fax: 0086-771-21899898
> E-mail: naft@aliyun.com

Unit 1 Structure and Layout of Business English Correspondence

> 83 SOI EKACHAI
> 66/6 EKACHAI ROAD
> BANGBON DISTRICT
> BANGKOK 10150, THAILAND
> Tel: 0066-28989887
> Fax: 0066-24171642
> E-mail: tsdrice@hotmail.com
> Website: http://www.tsdrice.com/

2. The Date

Though there is an automatic record of detailed date and time for online communication through social networking websites, date is very important in a business letter, because only a dated letter has legal force, and an undated letter has no legal force/authority. Therefore, a clear and definite expression of date should be added in a business letter. It is generally put two or three lines below the letterhead. The date line may start from the left margin, or be centered, or appear on the right-hand side, written in the order of day, month, year (British practice) or month, day, year (American practice). Do not use figures for the month and never give the date in figures (e.g. 8/2/2023), which causes confusion. These two styles are strongly advisable: 2 August, 2023 (British practice) and August 2, 2023 (American practice).

Of course, such styles as 12th July, 2023 or July 1st, 2023 sometimes are used, but they are somewhat old-fashioned. If the date figure is larger than 12, the form of 2023/07/18 is acceptable.

3. The Inside Name and Address

The inside name and address are the recipient's name and address, located two line-spacing below the date. Here, the recipient's name can be the person's courtesy title (only for a formal letter), personal name, executive title or the company name and the address refers to the mailing address.

The commonly used courtesy titles are "Mr.", "Ms." (used for all women, married or unmarried, especially for career women), "Mrs.", "Miss", and "Messrs." (used only for companies or firms named after a person or more persons).

Here come the examples of the inside name and address as below:

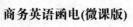

```
Mr. Smith
Hewlett-Packard (Canada) Co.
5150 Spectrum Way
Mississauga, Ontario L4W 5G1
Canada
```

```
Joe Martin
First Trucking
5656 North Willow Road
Middleton, NY 20088
```

4. The Salutation

The salutation is a greeting to the recipient which every letter begins with. Always it flushes with the left margin two lines below the inside name and address. We usually use these salutations accordingly: "Dear Sir/Madam", "Dear Sirs/Madams", (British practice), "Ladies and Gentlemen" or "Gentlemen" (American practice), "Dear Director/Supervisor". All these are used when you write to someone(s) unknown, but, to a specific person, we often use "Dear Mr./Mrs./Miss/Ms. …", or just "Dear Ann".

5. The Body / The Message

The body is the most important part of a letter. It is the message that the writer has to convey to the reader. The body is usually made up of three parts: (1) The opening paragraph refers to previous correspondence. (2) The middle paragraphs give more details, ask questions, present points of view, etc. (3) The closing paragraph is a statement of your intentions, hopes or expectations concerning the next step or for further contact. Sentences like "I am writing this letter to…", "We have your name and address from…", "We have received your letter of July 26, 2023…", etc. can often be found in the opening paragraph; and "Looking forward to your early reply", "Upon receipt of your specific inquiry, we will send you the samples and catalogs" or "Your favorable reply will be highly appreciated", etc. are usually used as closing sentences. The middle paragraphs are the most important in the letter, which must direct to the point, clear, concrete, and complete.

6. The Complimentary Close

The complimentary close refers to a formal closing sentence used to express thanks, wishes or

Unit 1 Structure and Layout of Business English Correspondence

other polite words to the recipient at the end of a letter or official letter. This part is usually written starting from the middle right part of the next or two lines of the text, and the first letter needs to be capitalized, and a comma is used at the end of the sentence. This polite way of closing helps demonstrate respect and professionalism and can enhance the formal feel of the letter. It is purely a matter of custom and a polite way of bringing a letter to an end. However, the expression of this part must suit the occasion and match the salutation. The widely used salutations with their matching complimentary close are shown in the table below.

Table 1 Salutation and the Matching Complimentary Close

Salutation	Complimentary Close	Salutation	Complimentary Close
Dear Sir/Madam Dear Sirs/Madams	Yours faithfully Faithfully yours Yours respectfully	Dear Mr. Smith Dear Ms. Smith Dear Dr. Smith	Yours sincerely Sincerely yours Cordially yours
Ladies/Gentlemen	Yours truly Truly yours	Dear Mary Dear Tom	Sincerely Cordially Best regards

7. The Signature

A letter should be signed by hand, and in ink, because only a signed letter has legal force and an unsigned letter has no legal force or authority. The signature block contains the handwritten signature of the writer, the full-typed name and sometimes the title of the writer. It often appears several lines beneath the complimentary close. The company name is also needed when the letter represents a company policy, position, or decision; and the company name should be typed entirely, usually in all capitals two lines below the complimentary close.

The commonly used signature is usually arranged as follows:

>Yours sincerely,
>
>Black G.L. Trading Co., Ltd.
>
>*Scott G. White* (handwritten name of the writer)
>
>Scott G. White (the writer's typed name)
>
>Director (job title of the writer)
>
>Sales Department (optional, name of the writer's division or department)

If the writer performs a task to write the letter on behalf of someone else, the signature is a little different, and words like "Per pro.", "By", "Per", or "For" will have to be added before the company name or the name of the person in a responsible position, as shown below:

    Yours sincerely,

    Per pro. HOPKINS & WRIGHT CO., LTD.

    Helen Brown (sgd.)

    Helen Brown

1.2.2 The Optional Parts

Except the above mentioned seven principle parts, there are six optional parts of a business letter. The six optional parts include:

- Reference Number
- Attention Line
- Subject Line
- Carbon Copy Notation
- Enclosure Notation
- Postscript

1. Reference Number

Reference number is typically used to identify a specific project, document, order, or other entity for tracking and management within an organization. This number is usually unique and can be used to quickly find and identify relevant information. For example, in a bank, each account has a unique reference number that distinguishes different accounts.

In business correspondence writing, reference number is often made to link replies with previous correspondence and helps for filing purposes. It usually includes a file number and should be positioned immediately below the letterhead marked with "Our ref." or "Your ref.", just like "**Your ref: CNN / 266**", "**Our ref: 1246 / BD**".

2. Attention Line

The attention line in a business correspondence refers to the information about the specific person in charge who handles the business. For example, in a document, form or contract, it may be necessary to designate a specific person to be responsible for handling or performing related tasks or responsibilities. This part exists to ensure that all important matters have a clear responsible person so that they can be held accountable or contacted when needed.

The attention line is used when the writer of a letter addressed to an organization wishes to

Unit 1　Structure and Layout of Business English Correspondence

direct the letter to a particular person or department who takes care of the business. It is put below the inside name and address, sometimes underlined. If there is an attention line on the stationery, there should also be one on the envelope. The attention line usually takes the following forms:

- Attention: Mr. …
- ATTENTION OF MR. …
- <u>For the attention of Mr. …</u>
- Attention: Marketing Director
- ATTN: Sales Manager/Mr. … (most often used at present)

3. Subject Line (often used)

　　The subject line of a letter or e-mail provides a concise summary of the message's content. Its main function is to help the recipients quickly understand the subject and focus of the e-mail, so that they can decide whether they need to read or process it immediately. In business letters, the "Subject Line" usually fills in the subject content of the letter, such as "Firm Offer", "Purchase Order", "Packing Proposal", etc. A clear and specific subject line can give the recipient a preliminary understanding of the content of the e-mail, and sometimes they can handle it accordingly without even opening the e-mail. Therefore, whether you are writing a letter or sending an e-mail, you should try to make the subject line concise and clear, and accurately reflect the main content of the e-mail or the letter.

　　Do remember that if a subject has already been used by your correspondent, your reply should carry the same subject. The subject line is often located below the salutation in such different forms as follows:

- Re: Rare Earth
- Subject: Your Contract No. TD1708
- <u>*Sub: Delay of Shipment*</u>
- <u>Re: Your Order No. LS 1786</u>

4. Carbon Copy

　　Carbon copy is a term for e-mail communication that means sending a message simultaneously to someone other than the recipient. When writing an e-mail to someone you can choose to use the "C.C." option. In this way, in addition to the primary recipient, other recipients you specify also can see the message. Carbon copy originates from the early method of copying with toner.

Carbon copy is put below the signature or enclosure notation at the left margin, followed by the name(s) of the person(s) who will receive copies of the letter. There are two forms: (1) C.C. (carbon copy: typed both on the original and copies of the letter.) and (2) B.C.C. (blind carbon copy: typed only on the copy/copies of the letter.), just shown as follows:

C.C.: Sam Ford, Susan Bush, Bill Owens

C.C.: Mr. Weber Carl, Vice-President

B.C.C.: H.R. Manager

5. Enclosure Notation (often used)

When there is something enclosed with the letter, we use "Enclosure" (or Attachment for an e-mail letter) below the identification marks or signature or carbon copy notation. It is useful to remind the sender to include it when folding/sending the letter and to help the receiver to check whether there is an enclosure in the letter. The enclosure has the following styles:

- Encls: 2 Price Lists
- Enclosures (2)
- Encl. 1 catalog
- Attachment: a/s (as stated)
- Encls. (3)
  2 Blank order forms
  1 Product catalog

6. Postscript (P.S.)

A postscript is used to draw the recipient's attention to the important information that is added or to clarify one last convincing argument for emphatic inclusion that the writer withholds. A postscript is an afterthought, and it is usually regarded as a sign of poor planning or carelessness. It should be avoided as far as possible. If it has to be used, put it below whatever has been written as "P.S. We are sending you under separate cover a copy of our latest catalogue", "P.S. Please send all the material by air mail", "P.S. Looking forward to seeing you at the trade fair on August 12", etc.

In practice, all these parts mentioned above are usually placed in the letter in such a way as shown below.

Unit 1　Structure and Layout of Business English Correspondence

Table 2　The Placement of Different Parts in a Business Letter

---

(1) Letterhead 信头

(2) Ref No. 文档编号/参考号

　　　　　　　　　　　　　　　　　　(3) Date 日期

(4) Inside Name & Address 信内名称和地址

(5) Attention Line 注意事项/经办人栏目

(6) Salutation 称呼

(7) Subject Line 事由标题

(8) Message or Body 信文

_____

_____

_____

_____

(9) Complimentary Close 结尾敬语

(10) Signature 签字

(11) Enclosure 附件

(12) Postscript 附言

(13) Carbon Copy 抄送

1.3　The Layout of Business Letters

The layout of a business letter should be clear, concise, and professional in order to convey the message and leave a good impression.

1.3.1　The Styles of Business Letters

There are many forms of business letters and here only the three most popular forms: full-block style, indented style and modified block style, will be illustrated.

1. Full-block Style

The full-block style, also known as complete justification or full justification, is a type of text alignment where every line of a paragraph is stretched to fill the entire width of the block or page.

In this style, both the left and right margins of each line are evenly aligned with the left and right margins of the block or page. This creates a clean and organized appearance, but it can sometimes make the text harder to read if there are long words or sentences that do not fit properly within the available space.

The full-block style is now the most widely used method of display for all business documents. This layout of this type reduces typing time as there are no indentations for new paragraphs or the closing section. All parts, though sometimes the letterhead is placed in the center, are placed against the left-hand margin. The following sample letter is a good illustration.

Sample Letter 1

Nanning ASEAN Fruit Trading Co., Ltd.

100 Youyi Road, Qingxiu District

Nanning 530022, P. R. China

Tel: 0086-771-21899899   Fax: 0086-771-21899898

E-mail: naft@aliyun.com

July 12th, 2023

Our Ref.

Your Ref.

G.W. First F&V Trading Company

5826 North Willow Road

Middletown, NY 20088

U.S.A.

ATTN: Purchasing Manager

Dear Sirs,

Subject: Establishing Business Relations

Unit 1 Structure and Layout of Business English Correspondence

> We learned from Alibaba.com that you are in the market for Asian fruit. We have been a supplier in this line of business for many years. We are writing to establish business relations with you.
>
> Further information will be available on your request. We are awaiting your prompt reply.
>
> Yours faithfully,
>
> *Delia Wang*
> Delia Wang
> Sales Manager
>
> C.C.: Sam Ford, Susan Bush, Bill Owens
>
> Encl. 1 catalogue
>
> P.S.: We will send all the materials and samples by air mail.

2. Indented Style

It is a traditional letter format, particularly British style. The characteristic of this format is that the beginning of each paragraph is indented a certain distance to the right, thus forming a neat structure. Specifically, each line of text in the letterhead and the inside address will be indented by one or two letters to the right compared to the previous line. The first line of each paragraph of text will also be indented by four letters to the right. However, although this format was once very popular, it has largely fallen out of use.

Nowadays, if used, the date, complimentary close and signature are on the right, with the letterhead and the subject line in the middle of the page. See the following sample letter for vivid illustration.

Sample Letter 2

Nanning ASEAN Fruit Trading Co., Ltd.

100 Youyi Road, Qingxiu District

Nanning 530022, P. R. China

Tel: 0086-771-21899899

Fax: 0086-771-21899898

E-mail: naft@aliyun.com

July 12th, 2023

Our Ref.

Your Ref.

G.W. First F&V Trading Company

5826 North Willow Road

Middletown, NY 20088

U.S.A.

ATTN: Purchasing Manager

Dear Sirs,

Subject: Establishing Business Relations

  We learned from Alibaba.com that you are in the market for Asian fruit. We have been a supplier in this line of business for many years. We are writing to establish business relations with you.

  Further information will be available on your request. We are awaiting your prompt reply.

Yours faithfully,

Delia Wang

Delia Wang

Sales Manager

C.C.: Sam Ford, Susan Bush, Bill Owens

Unit 1　Structure and Layout of Business English Correspondence

> Encl. 1 catalogue
>
> P.S.: We will send all the materials and samples by air mail.

3. Modified Block Style

Modified Block style combines the characteristics of left and right alignment. In this format, each line of the text in the letterhead, date, and inside address is indented a certain distance to the right, while each paragraph of text in the body is aligned left. In addition, compared with Block Style, Modified Block Style has proper spacing and a more beautiful text layout. This format is characterized by easy reading and clear text organization, so it is widely used in letter writing in the business and engineering fields.

Usually, in practice, in this style, all parts are placed against the left-hand margin except the complimentary close and signature on the right, while the subject line is in the middle of the page, which can be well illustrated in the following sample letter.

Sample Letter 3

> **Nanning ASEAN Fruit Trading Co., Ltd.**
> 100 Youyi Road, Qingxiu District
> Nanning 530022, P. R. China
> Tel: 0086-771-21899899
> Fax: 0086-771-21899898
> E-mail: naft@aliyun.com
> July 12th, 2023
> Our Ref.
> Your Ref.
>
> G.W. First F&V Trading Company
> 5826 North Willow Road
> Middletown, NY 20088
> U.S.A.

ATTN: Purchasing Manager

Dear Sirs,

<u>Subject: Establishing Business Relations</u>

We learned from Alibaba.com that you are in the market for Asian fruit. We have been a supplier in this line of business for many years. We are writing to establish business relations with you.

Further information will be available on your request. We are awaiting your prompt reply.

Yours faithfully,

Delia Wang

Delia Wang

Sales Manager

C.C.: Sam Ford, Susan Bush, Bill Owens

Encl. 1 catalogue

P.S.: We will send all the materials and samples by air mail.

1.3.2　Envelopes Addressing

There are three essentials of envelope addressing, i.e. accuracy, clearness and good appearance. The sender's name and address should always be put in the upper left corner of the envelope, while the recipient's name and address above half way down the envelope from the center, leaving enough space for the postmark and stamps. Post notations such as "Registered", "Certified", or "Confidential" should be placed in the bottom left-hand corner. The following examples are good illustrations.

Unit 1 Structure and Layout of Business English Correspondence

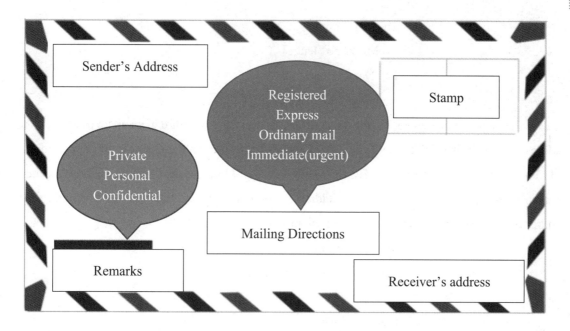

Figure 1 The Placement of Relevant Information on an Envelope

Figure 2 The Placement of Sender's and Recipient's Information on an Envelope

When a letter is mailed to a third person who is bound to pass it onto the addressee, write the third person's name with the words "care of" in front of it down below the addressee's name, followed by this third person's address, as shown below:

Mr. Paul Smith

c/o Mr. Zhao Heng

128 Daxue Road

Nanning, 530001 Guangxi, China

If the letter, not mailed by the post office, is trusted to a third person to pass onto the addressee, words like "By Politeness of / By Kindness of / Through the Courtesy of / Per Kindness of / Forwarded by / Per Favor of / By (or With) Favor of / Favored by" are put before this third person's name, after the name of the addressee, or only "Please Forward" is put before the addressee's name. The following examples can provide good details:

Mr. Paul Smith

Kindness of Mr. Zhao Heng

Please Forward

Mr. Paul Smith

Useful Words & Expressions

I. Widely-used Terms

1. salutation	称呼	2. inside name & address	封内姓名、地址
3. attention line	经办人栏目	4. reference number	参考编号，引用编号
5. carbon copy	抄送	6. subject line	信件或电子邮件的标题
7. attachment	附件(电子邮件)	8. complimentary close	(信件)结尾敬语
9. product catalog	产品目录	10. blank order forms	空白订单表格
11. sample book	样品册	12. cotton piece goods	棉布
13. the full-block style	完全齐头式	14. the indented style	缩进式
15. registered	挂号(信件)	16. modified block style	改良齐头式
17. certified	(邮寄)证书	18. confidential	绝密(信件)

II. Important Phrases

1. in the market for	想要购买
2. in this line of	在这一行业

Unit 1 Structure and Layout of Business English Correspondence

3. further information	详细信息
4. be desirous of sth.	想要某物
5. deal in	经营
6. establish business relations	建立贸易关系
7. one of the leading dealers	最主要的经销商之一
8. on your request	应你方要求

Exercises

I. Arrange the following elements in proper form as they should be set out in a letter.

1. Sender's name: Shenzhen Sunfun Import & Export Trading Co.

2. Sender's address: 207 Dongmen Road, Futian District, Shenzhen, China

3. Sender's telephone number: + 86-0755-82541332

4. Sender's Fax: + 86-0755-82541332

5. Date: June 18th, 2023

6. Recipient's name: John and Tony

7. Recipient's address: 58 Sixth Avenue, New York, America

8. Salutation: Dear Sirs,

9. Subject Matter: Mobile Phone Shell

10. The message:

We have received your letter of May 20th. As requested, we are enclosing our catalogue and under separate cover we are sending you our samples, which will help you in your selection.

We are looking forward to your early reply.

11. Complimentary close: Yours faithfully,

Signature: Shenzhen Sunfun Trading Co., Manager: Wang Wei

12. Enc. As Stated.

13. C.C. to: ABC Company

II. Change the layout of the following letter into modified block style.

Sunshine Overseas Trading Co.

Friday Street

London E.C.4, England

Phone: +0044-2077029128   Fax: +0044-2077029128

E-mail: Sunshine@hotmail.com

January 10th, 2023

Beijing Beauty Textiles

Import & Export Corporation

56 Renmin Street

Haidian District

Beijing, China

Dear Sirs,

Men's T-shirts

We have obtained your contact information from Alibaba, *Textile Export & Import News Column* and are now writing to you for the establishment of business relations.

We are glad to learn from your advertisement that you are dealing in cotton piece goods. Now we are keenly desirous of enlarging our trade with Chinese companies. We are quite interested in your Men's T-shirts with Chinese elements.

We should appreciate it if you would send us your latest catalogue, price list and sample books. We are one of the leading dealers in textiles in our area and there is a large demand here for the goods of the kind mentioned. We shall place a large order with you if your products are good in quality and reasonable in price.

If you find business possible, please write to us.

Yours faithfully,

Sunshine Overseas Trading Co.

Steven Abel

General Manager

Unit 1 Structure and Layout of Business English Correspondence

III. Address the following envelope in English.

美国纽约第六大道 58 号 Big Apple 公司　　邮编：10452

　　　　　　　　　　　　约翰·安东尼先生 收

　　　　　　　　　　　　中国广东省深圳市福田区东门街 207 号

　　　　　　　　　　　　深圳三福进出口贸易公司

　　　　　　　　　　　　　　　邮编　518000

 微课视频

　　扫一扫，获取本课相关微课视频。

1.2.1　The Seven Principle　　1.2.2　The Optional Parts.mp4　　1.3　The Layout of Business
　　　　Parts.mp4　　　　　　　　　　　　　　　　　　　　　　　　Letters.mp4

Unit 2 Writing Principles

2.1 Introduction

The purpose of communication is to obtain complete understanding between the parties involved, and elicit the responses required. Different business letters about the same issue might bring about different results. Therefore, it is of vital importance for businessmen to master the skills of business writing, writing effective and productive business letters. The first step, needless to say, is to know the basic principles of writing a good business letter. Generally speaking, there are 7 Cs principles for the writing of the business letter, namely, courtesy, consideration, completeness, clarity, conciseness, concreteness and correctness.

When you write a business letter, you are trying to convince someone to act or react in a positive way. Your reader will respond quickly only if your meaning is crystal clear.

Show your interest in the reader's circumstances. If he/she has mentioned something personal in the letter, refer to it in your reply. This builds a bridge between you and the reader. Read the original letter carefully and see if there is something you can put in your letter to show your interest.

A well-written business letter could contribute to a company's image. If the letter is clear and concise, the firm seems well-organized and competent, which may ultimately bring about a lot of business. If the letter is courteous and considerate, it may help you eliminate the misunderstanding or divergence of views between you and your counterparts. Therefore, effective writing has become central to the success of a business and writing letters in English has become an important part of business professionals' daily work in companies of foreign concerns.

2.2　The Principles of Business Letter Writing

2.2.1　The Principle of Consideration

In business letter writing, consideration means keeping in mind the person you are writing to, understanding and respecting the recipient's point of view, seeing his/her problems and difficulties and expressing ideas in terms of his/her experience. So, consideration first stems from a sincere You-attitude.

Consideration requires a business letter to be written in the following ways:

1. Take the "You-attitude" Instead of "I/We-attitude"

Business writing requires the writer to "put yourself in the reader's shoes", and to put yourself in his/her place, considering his/her wishes, demands, interests and difficulties. So, keep this in your mind: when writing business letters, you should avoid a self-centered attitude focusing on your own concerns rather than those of the recipient; even if you must talk about yourself, do so in a way that relates your concerns to those of the recipient.

However, "You-attitude" does not always mean the use of "you, your, or yours"; this approach sometimes requires the use of "I/We, my/our, me/us, or mine/ours", especially when you have to hold someone for responsibility or the like.

The table below gives some examples to account for the above mentioned.

Table 3　You-attitude vs. We-attitude

You-attitude	We-attitude
You can earn 2 percent discount for cash payment.	We allow 2 percent discount for cash payment.
We are pleased to announce that…	You will be pleased to know that…
You will have a free customer service for your newly purchased refrigerator for 3 years.	We will offer you free customer service for your newly purchased refrigerator for 3 years.
To maintain your excellent credit reputation, please pay your overdue bill.	We are in need of funds and that's why your overdue bill must be paid right away.
You are welcome to rent our equipment on a cash rental basis.	We do not permit outside groups to use our equipment except on a cash rental basis.

2. Focus on the Positive Approach

Negative approach usually gives people a negative impression. Especially in the business world, people don't like negative words or expressions. However, we can't avoid negative news. Remember: when you have to convey or discuss something negative, try to take the positive approach and avoid such words as "cannot", "forbid", "fail", "impossible", "refuse", "prohibit", "restrict", and "deny" as much as possible. When you need to present negative information, soften its effects by superimposing a positive picture on a negative one.

Compare the following table, and you can see the advantage of positive approach.

Table 4　Positive Approach vs. Negative Approach

Positive	Negative
Your warranty begins working for you as soon as you return your owner's registration.	Our warranty becomes effective only when we receive an owner's registration.
We will send you the brochure next month.	We won't be able to send you the brochure this month.
We feel sure that you will be entirely satisfied with this order of pitayas.	We do not believe you will have cause for dissatisfaction with this order of pitayas.
To keep down packaging costs and to help customers save on shipping costs, we ship in lots of 12 or more.	We cannot ship in lots of less than 12.
You could obtain a refund if the goods you returned had remained clean and usable.	We cannot offer you any refunds if the goods you returned are dirty and unusable.

3. Employ Passive Voice

When you have to convey messages that use "you" might offend your reader in negative situations, employ the passive voice to depersonalize the situation. Passive voice can help to emphasize the matter and distract attention from the persons concerned. This can be illustrated by the following table.

Table 5　Passive Voice vs. Active Voice

Passive Voice	Active Voice
The pre-ordering was automatically canceled since the down payment was not received before 7:00 p.m.	Since you failed to make the down payment, we could not keep the goods for you after 7:00 p.m.
We regret that the goods can't be sent today.	We regret that we can't ship the goods today.
If the price can't be reduced, we will have to find other suppliers.	If you don't reduce the price, we will have to find other suppliers.
Another 3% price discount will be offered for orders amounting to USD50,000.	We offer another 3% price discount for orders amounting to USD50,000.
If the goods are out of stock, a refund will be made to you.	If the goods are out of stock, we will make you a refund.

2.2.2　The Principle of Courtesy

Courtesy is not mere politeness. Courtesy means showing tactfully in your letters the honest friendship, thoughtful appreciation, sincere politeness, considerate understanding and heartfelt respect. Courtesy helps to foster a positive relationship with your reader and is more likely to bring about a favorable response.

Following the principle of courtesy in a business letter, generally speaking, includes three aspects: being polite, being positive and being personal.

Courtesy means more than politeness. Courtesy≠politeness, instead, courtesy＞politeness. Real courtesy comes from the sincere "you" attitude. When writing a letter, keep the reader's requests, needs and desires in mind and try to convey to him/her your care and consideration. Of course, you should never use the rude expression in a commanding tone and always be prompt to give a reply.

1. Be Sincere, Tactful, Thoughtful and Appreciative

To be sincere, tactful, thoughtful and appreciative in your business writing, you can bring your readers nearer and enable a request to be refused without killing all hope of future business, or allow a refusal to perform a favor without killing a friendship. To apply this principle, you need to follow these ways:

(1) If an apology is necessary, make it courteously and sincerely;

(2) Use "I'm afraid", "Unfortunately", "However", etc., when you can't meet your recipient's requirements;

(3) Use imperative sentence such as "thank you for" to show your gratitude;

The following table is a very good illustration.

Table 6　Courtesy vs. Discourtesy

Discourtesy	Courtesy
You didn't find our durians are one of the most popular in the word.	We are sorry that you didn't find our durians are one of the most popular in the word.
We cannot deliver the goods all at one time.	I'm afraid we cannot deliver the goods all at one time.
We must tell you that we can't accept your price.	Unfortunately, we cannot accept your price.
We have received your order for 500 M/T mango.	Thank you for your order for 500 M/T mango.
You ought to have accepted the offer.	It seems to us that you ought to have accepted the offer.

2. Avoid Irritating, Offensive or Belittling Expressions

In foreign trade, the two parties are equal partners. Therefore, in order to make a business letter courteous, try to avoid irritating, offensive, or belittling statements. In a business letter the followings are very offensive and should never appear.

You are ignorant of the fact that…

You forgot that…

You leave us no choice…

You overlooked…

You should know…

You must…

We don't agree with you…

Why don't you…

To avoid irritating, offensive, or belittling statements, you need to remember these ways:

(1) When you find mistakes, errors, inappropriateness, ambiguousness, etc., use "if…" to correct them instead of just pointing out the problems.

(2) Use tactful expressions such as "Would you please… / May we suggest… / We should be obliged (glad) to… / We would appreciate it… / We would like (are pleased) to…", etc. to make suggestion.

The following table provides detailed examples as illustrations.

Table 7 Courtesy vs. Discourtesy

Discourtesy	Courtesy
Your letter does not clearly describe your detailed requirements of our assorted canned fruit, so I can't understand it.	If we can understand your letter correctly, we are able to give you a definite reply. Please refer to the catalog attached for information.
Tell me more detailed information on your requirements.	Would you tell us more detailed information on your requirements?
You are requested to remit the amount by August 10th.	Please remit the amount by August 10th.
We suggest that whenever you have any problem with our products you contact our after-sales service as soon as possible.	May we suggest that whenever you have any problem with our products you contact our after-sales service as soon as possible?

3. Be Prompt in Answering Letters

Courtesy also means giving immediate reply to the letter received. In the business world, time is money. Answer letters on the same day they are received if possible and write to explain why if you fail to do it promptly. Answering letters in good time will create a good impression and grasp more business opportunities.

2.2.3　The Principle of Conciseness

Conciseness means conveying all the necessary information with the fewest possible words without sacrificing clarity, courtesy, completeness and good expression. To achieve conciseness, you should explain your position in reasonably few words and avoid wordiness or redundancy. Besides, proper paragraphing is needed. Remember: long-winded writing can be annoying because unnecessary words, irrelevant details and muddled expressions waste the reader's time. To achieve conciseness, try to observe the following suggestions:

1. Use Words to Replace Phrases

A letter written with wordiness or redundancy will not be welcomed in the business circle. A good business letter should be precise and to the point. To avoid wordiness, when you can use one word, try to avoid using the phrase, as shown in table 8.

Table 8　Wordy Phrases vs. Words

Wordy Phrases	Words	Wordy Phrases	Words
conduct a discussion of	discuss	in the matter of	about
give consideration to	consider	due to the fact that	because
engage in the preparation of	prepare	for the reason that	since/because
make a discovery of	discover	in due course	timely/soon
make an assumption of	assume	during the year that	during
in the event that	if	at this time	now

Here are more examples for enlightenment:

(1) **Wordy:** Enclosed herewith please find two catalogues of our dried longan and litchi.

Concise: We enclose two catalogues of our dried longan and litchi.

(2) **Wordy:** Will you be good enough to let us know the results as soon as possible?

Concise: Please let us know the results as soon as possible.

(3) **Wordy:** In compliance with your request, we immediately contacted ABC Co., Ltd, and now wish to inform you of the result as follows.

Concise: As requested we immediately contacted ABC Co., Ltd., with the following result.

2. Use Daily Expressions to Replace Jargon

Stereotyped phrases and out-of-date commercial jargon do nothing good to the business letter but to make it ambiguous and hard to understand. So, try to express your idea in brief modern English.

Compare the following groups of sentences:

(1) **Wordy:** We take the liberty to approach you with the request that you would be kind enough to introduce to us some importers of agricultural products in your country.

Concise: Please introduce to us some importers of agricultural products in your country.

(2) **Wordy:** Enclosed herewith please find two price lists of our dried longan and litchi.

Concise: We have enclosed two price lists of our dried longan and litchi.

(3) **Wordy:** The contract enclosed herewith requires your signature before it can be executed and should be directed to the undersigned.

Concise: Please sign the contract enclosed and return it to me.

(4) **Wordy:** I hope you will be in a position to make a decision within a short time.

Concise: I hope you can decide soon.

3. Avoid Unnecessary Repeat

A repeated word can make the whole information boring. Sometimes repetition is necessary in order to lay focus on particular information, but this should not be practiced without more than one reason. In order to avoid redundancy, do not use two words with the same meaning in the same sentence.

A number of common phrases in our language actually say the same thing two or more times, but we sometimes don't even notice they are redundant, because these phrases are so common. Please see the examples below:

(1) **Wordy:** We have begun to export our machines to the foreign countries.

Concise: We have begun to export our machines.

(2) **Wordy:** Will you ship us any time during the month of December, or even November if you are rushed, for November would suit us just as well?

Concise: Please ship us in November or December.

(3) **Wordy:** We wish to acknowledge receipt of your letter of May 2nd with the check for $200 enclosed and wish to thank you for the same.

Concise: We appreciate your letter of May 2nd and the check for $200 you sent with it.

Here are more examples of the same kind.

Table 9 Redundant Phrases vs. Concise Words

Redundant Phrases	Concise Words
advance planning	planning
merge together	merge
important essentials	essentials
true facts	facts
past history	history
end results	results

4. Paragraph Correctly, Confining Each Paragraph to One Topic

As a whole, conciseness in business writing should be seen in paragraphs. A concise letter should control the number of the words, and build effective sentences and paragraphs. To apply conciseness to writing, the writer is suggested bearing these in mind:

(1) Use a short opening and a short closing;

(2) Include only relevant facts;

(3) Confine each paragraph to one idea.

2.2.4 The Principle of Clarity

Clarity means using plain, simple language appropriate to the understanding level of your reader. Good, straightforward, simple English is what clarity needs for business letters.

People do not want to waste time reading long, wordy letters with unclear message. To write your business letters effectively, you should avoid using, as far as possible, roundabout, old-fashioned phrases that add nothing to the sense of your message. Plain, simple words will be more easily understood than long elaborate phrases. The letter should express meaning clearly to make the reader understand it well. To achieve this, the writer should try to:

1. Avoid Using Polysemous/Homographic Words

Polysemous words bear more than one meaning. Though from the context, readers can get the meaning, it is not direct and not on the side as business letters; what's more, sometimes the reader can't get the exact meaning even if he/she analyzes the context. But for homographic words, the readers are usually completely puzzled. The following sentence is a vivid example:

E.g.:

In this season, we have bimonthly direct services from Victoria to Rotterdam...

The port "Victoria" can be called a homographic word, because there are as many as 21 Victoria ports in the world and most of them are suitable for international shipment, such as in Hong Kong China, Canada, Brazil, Guinea, Chile, Malta, Seychelles, etc. "Bimonthly" has two meanings: twice a month, or once two months. So, the reader will feel puzzled about the meaning. The sentence must be rewritten as the followings accordingly:

(1) In this season, we have <u>semimonthly direct services</u> from <u>Victoria, HK</u> to Rotterdam.

(2) In this season, we have <u>two direct services every month</u> from <u>Victoria, CA</u> to Rotterdam.

(3) In this season, we have direct services from <u>Victoria, GN</u> to Rotterdam <u>every two months</u>.

2. Pay Attention to the Position of Modifiers

Modifiers are frequently used in business letters to emphasize or highlight an idea or something. The same modifier will lead to different implications and functions when it is put in different positions of the sentence and careless use of modifiers results in misunderstanding and hard-to-read sentences. The following examples can well illustrate it.

E.g.:

(1) For this product, we can accept orders <u>only</u> above 5000 M/T now.

(2) <u>Only</u> for this product, we can accept orders above 5000 M/T now.

(3) For this product, <u>only</u> we can accept orders above 5000 M/T now.

(4) For this product, we can accept orders above 5000 M/T <u>only</u> now.

The modifier "only" in the above sentences is put in different places to modify four different words, so the four sentences have different meanings. Thus, the practical principle for using modifiers is to put the modifiers as close as possible to the word or words they are modifying. This is the idea of keeping related words together and as close as possible. This principle is applicable to all modifiers. Read more examples below:

E.g.:

(1) <u>Our</u> black plum is the most popular with European customers.

(2) Black plum is <u>our</u> most popular with European customers.

(3) Black plum is the most popular with <u>our</u> European customers.

In fact, adjectival possessive pronouns or adjectives should be placed right next to the things they describe, and adverbs should be placed right next to the action or the other modifiers they describe.

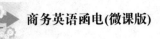

2.2.5　The Principle of Concreteness

Concreteness means making your message specific, definite and vivid rather than vague, general and abstract. A business letter should avoid emptiness in contents and vagueness in ideas. Any ambiguous or vague words must be avoided and the information must be supplied with definiteness and concreteness.

Giving your recipient specific facts and definite figures helps to show your sincerity for cooperation and the actual strength of your company.

For example, some qualities or characters of goods should be shown with exact figures or facts and avoid words like "short", "long" or "good". The following groups of sentences are very good examples for us to make a comparison.

E.g.:

(1) **Vague:** Various aspects of this equipment make it a good choice.

Concrete: This machine is a good choice because it is more compact and less expensive than any other one in the market.

(2) **Vague:** Our dried starfruit is of high quality but much cheaper than other suppliers'.

Concrete: Our dried starfruit is larger, drier, and sweeter but much 5% lower in price than other suppliers'.

(3) **Vague:** Sales of our mangosteens skyrocketed last month.

Concrete: Sales of our mangosteens increased 10 percent last month.

Giving specific time (with date, month, year and even offer hour, minute if necessary) and important document number to reference can make your recipient assured of the trade and help you gain more chances. So, try to avoid expressions such as "yesterday, next month, immediately, soon, as usual", etc. The following groups of sentences can illustrate this very well.

E.g.:

(1) **Vague:** We will ship your order soon.

Concrete: We will ship the pawpaws you ordered July 9 by Ocean Prince on July 30th.

(2) **Vague:** We have drawn on you as usual under your L/C.

Concrete: We have drawn on you our sight draft No. 845 for the Invoice amount, US $560.00, under your L/C No. 246 of the China Bank.

2.2.6 The Principle of Correctness

Correctness is a must for business correspondence. Correct grammar, punctuation and spelling are basic requirements for business letter writing. Correctness refers not only to the correct usage of grammar, punctuation and spelling, but also to standard language and proper statement. Business letters must contain factual information, accurate figures and exact terms in particular, for they involve the rights, the duties and the interest of both parties. It is the basis of all commercial documents (such as the contract, the letter of credit, etc.). Therefore we should neither understate nor overstate as understatement might lead to less confidence and hold up the trade development, while overstatement throws you into an awkward position.

Whenever you are writing letters, you must check the typings of figures, types or models of goods, specifications and quantity required etc. again and again before sending them out in order not to make any mistakes which will bring injuries to your business.

Here are the practical ways of applying correctness in the letter:

(1) Use the correct level of language;

(2) Include only accurate facts, terms, words and figures;

(3) Maintain acceptable writing mechanics;

(4) Apply all other relevant "C" principles.

2.2.7 The Principle of Completeness

A business letter is complete when it contains all the necessary information. A complete business letter can bring the desired results, build goodwill between the buyer and the seller and help avoid costly lawsuits. On the contrary, incomplete information is annoying and costly because it holds up business transactions and duplicates work.

To strive for completeness, keep the following guidelines in mind:

1. Write down all the points you wish to cover and then arrange them in a logical order.

2. If your letter is a reply, underline those parts which seek for information and answer all the questions asked.

3. Give something extra, when desirable.

4. Check for the 5 Ws (Who, What, When, Where, Why) and any other writing principles.

Though we have discussed the employment of 7 Cs writing principles to be followed in business English correspondence writing here, it should be noted that, in some way, there is no complete separation among some of them. In other words, some of them overlap with each other in some degree or in some aspects. Anyway, when writing business correspondence, we should bear in our minds the principles and follow them appropriately and flexibly.

Useful Words & Expressions

I. Widely-used Terms

1. cash payment	现金支付	2. overdue bill	逾期汇票/账单
3. cash rental	现金租赁	4. refund	退款
5. down payment	首付款、定金	6. out of stock	无现货、缺货
7. credit reputation	信用声誉	8. remit the amount	汇款
9. the brochure	(商品)宣传册		

II. Important Phrases

1. free customer service —— 免费客户服务
2. keep down the cost —— 降低开支
3. after-sales service —— 售后服务
4. You-attitude / We-attitude —— 以你/我方为中心；替你/我方着想
5. the principle of consideration —— 体谅原则
6. put yourself in his/her place —— 设身处地为……着想
7. account for —— 解释；说明
8. positive/negative approach —— 积极/消极方式
9. in lots of less than 12 —— 少于十二件(货物)
10. be out of stock —— 缺货
11. the principle of courtesy —— 礼貌原则
12. the principle of conciseness —— 简洁性原则
13. wordy phrase —— 冗长的短语
14. jargon —— 行话
15. enclosed herewith please find —— 随函附上，请查收
16. be in a position to do… —— 能够做……
17. redundant phrase —— 冗余短语
18. the principle of clarity —— 清晰性原则

19. polysemous/homographic words 多义词/同形词
20. the principle of concreteness 具体性原则
21. overlap with each other 相互重叠

Exercises

I. Answer the following questions according to what has been learned in this unit.

What are the 7 Cs principles for the writing of business letters? And what are their Chinese equivalents?

II. Point out the principle used in the following sentences.

1. I am writing to you at the suggestion of the Import & Export Trade Association's office in your country.

2. These new 3D Printers type 120 fairly clear pictures in one minute.

3. You should receive by July 8th the cotton Men's T-shirts you ordered on June 28th.

4. Thanks for your letter of February 13th, in which you expressed your interest in Blanket Cover (No. 1056).

5. Please let us know your latest CIF Shanghai prices, together with your terms of payment and the earliest delivery date.

III. Improve the following sentences according to the writing principles in the bracket.

1. Apparently you have forgotten what I wrote to you two weeks ago. (Courtesy)

2. I am writing to ask for some basic information about your product. (Clarity)

3. I need your response immediately so that I can arrange the shipment with the carrier by next week. (Consideration)

4. At this time I am writing to you to establish business relations with your company for the purpose of introducing our new products which has a high public praise in other areas for a long time. (Conciseness)

5. We take the liberty to introduce our dried longan as the best-selling goods to you which is of high quality but much cheaper than other suppliers'. (Concreteness)

微课视频

扫一扫,获取本课相关微课视频。

2　Writing Principles.mp4

Unit 3　Establishing Business Relations

3.1　Background Knowledge

3.1.1　Case Study

1. Case One

Suppose you are the salesperson of ABC Company, dealing with dairy products. You want to sell your products to an overseas company. Now you are writing a letter to release information on www.alibaba.com. What would you write in order to sell the products?

2. Case Two

From the following letter, what information can you get? Please use some key words to summarize the information you get from the following letter.

To: "Sales Department" <abccompany@hotmail.com>
From: "Delia" <sunnynutritiousfoodinc@gmail.com>
Subject: Establishing Business Relationship

Dear Sirs,

We have obtained your name and address from the website: www.alibaba.com, learning that you are one of the biggest exporters of canned food in China. We take this opportunity to approach you in the hope of establishing business relations with you.

We are one of the leading importers of canned vegetables and fruit in America and would like you to send us your latest price list and illustrated catalogues as well as some information about such items available for export now.

Looking forward to your early reply.

Yours faithfully,

Delia Wang

Purchasing Manager

3.1.2 Relevant Information

International trade firms/enterprises, either newly-founded or well-established, need to maintain or expand their business activities, so they should have a lot of overseas business connections. In order to enter into business relations with foreign firms, the trade firms/enterprises should write correspondence to express their desire to trade with the potential partners on certain terms and conditions. This is the first step in our import and export business.

1. The Importance of Establishing Business Relations

Establishing business relations with prospective customers actually means choosing and determining the trade partner. It is the first step to develop trade ties. Business growth and expansion largely depend on the establishment of business relations. Generally, the two parties are introduced by themselves or by a third party.

2. The Source Channels

With the development of information technology, information channels are playing a more and more important role in international trade. We can even say whoever gets or releases the information first grasps the larger opportunity to win out. The most widely used channels through which the prospective dealers abroad may approach others or may be approached are illustrated as follows:

(1) Advertisement in the newspaper, from broadcast, TV and through the Internet;

(2) Introduction from business connections and mutual visits by trade delegations or groups;

(3) Internet websites;

(4) Market investigations;

(5) Attendance at the export commodities fairs or exhibitions;

(6) A chamber of commerce. A chamber of commerce is an organization of businessmen. One of its tasks is to get business information and to find new business opportunities for its members;

(7) Trade directory;

(8) Self-introductions or enquiries received from the merchants abroad;

(9) Banks;

(10) Commercial Counselor's Office in foreign countries;

(11) Foreign Commercial Counselor's Office in China.

3. The Steps in Establishing Business Relations

As international trade companies, in order to enter into business relationships with the potential partners, you should usually follow these steps:

Firstly, get the names and addresses of the firms you want to do business with through one or more than one of the above source channels. Find out those whose line of business coincides with yours.

Secondly, make "Status Inquiries" by writing to your bank, any chambers of commerce or inquiry agencies to get all the necessary information about the financial position, credit, reputation and business methods of the firms you are going to deal with.

Finally, if your "Status Inquiries" turn out to be satisfactory, then send a letter to the firm concerned to build up trade relations with, which is usually referred to as "First Inquiry".

3.1.3 Writing Skills

1. Writing Skills of Seeking New Clients Letters

To seek new clients, the writer should make him/her known to the potential clients first, leaving an attractive cooperative impression. Letters with this purpose should follow these skills:

(1) Conciseness: Get to the point at the very beginning, presenting the most important information, not everything, of your company to arouse others' interest in cooperating with you.

(2) Sincerity: Show your strength with a down-to-earth attitude to conduct business, not holding your head high, not boasting.

(3) Completeness: Make sure you have made an overall preface of your business intention with as few words as possible.

2. Writing Skills of Establishing Business Relations Letters

Having learned about the business intention of the potential partner, the businessperson will write a letter in the hope of establishing business relations. The following skills are useful for this kind of letters.

(1) **Conciseness:** Write a short letter of no more than one page and get to the point in the opening paragraph.

(2) **Courtesy:** Write in polite language, with courteous and sincere attitude.

(3) **Encouragement:** Speak highly of your company/products and list some well-known customers, if any.

3.2　Sample Letters and Basic Writing Structure Analysis

3.2.1　Basic Writing Structures of Seeking New Clients Letters

In order to expand business or enter into a new market, a company needs constantly to search for new trading partners and renew business relationships. To make this business intention known to the potential clients, the company will use different information transmission modes to launch the information and letters are one of the most widely accepted mode. Such letters always include the following parts:

1. A brief self-introduction, including the company's strength, business scope, products, integrity or reputation and other necessary information;

2. The intention or desire to seek business deals;

3. An expression of expectation to cooperate with the potential clients.

Letter 1　Seeking New Clients

To: Those who are concerned **From:** "Wilson" <shqfoodcompany@hotmail.com> **Subject:** Seeking New Clients
Dear Sirs, Established in 1998, Safe Healthy Quality Food Company is one of the largest experienced food trading companies in China with offices or representatives in all major cities in the country. We specialize in canned food, such as canned fruit, canned vegetables, canned meat, canned fruit cocktail, and by-products. All our products are strictly inspected to meet the standards for export.

Unit 3　Establishing Business Relations

We have been exporting a large variety of canned foods to Europe.

We are writing this letter in the hope of serving you with our professional experience from now on. We would like to offer you the fast-moving consumer goods with best price. Please feel free to contact us. Samples and more information are available for you anytime.

We are looking forward to our cooperation in the near future.

Yours faithfully,

Wilson

Sales Manager

3.2.2　Basic Writing Structures of Letters About Establishing Business Relations

When receiving letters asked to enter into business relationship, generally, the recipient will reply immediately to express willingness. The letter usually contains the following information:

1. The source of the information, i.e., how and where the writer has got the name and the address of the addressee's company;

2. The intention or desire to establish business relations;

3. A brief self-introduction, including the business scope, branches, financial status, integrity of the writer's company and other necessary information;

4. The writer's expectation of cooperation between the two parties.

Letter 2　Request for Establishing Business Relations

To: "Wilson" <shqfoodcompany@hotmail.com>
From: "Delia" <sunnynutritiousfoodinc@gmail.com>
Subject: Establishing Business Relationship

Dear Wilson,

We learned from www.alibaba.com that you are a leading exporter of Chinese canned food, which falls within our business line. We take the liberty of writing this letter in the hope of opening account with you.

We are glad to introduce ourselves as an established food importer with business contact in more than 30 countries, handling food import for more than 40 years. Assorted canned vegetables, canned fishery and canned grapes in syrup are most popular with our customers.

We would be greatly appreciated for your latest catalogue, brochure and price list. We would also expect to receive your free sample before the trial order is placed.

We are awaiting your prompt reply.

Yours faithfully,

Delia

Purchasing Manager

3.2.3　Basic Writing Structures of Letters About Credit Inquiry

Before establishing business relations with a new client, in order to avoid or lower the risk of non-payment or non-delivery, the seller or the buyer will write credit inquiry letters to the correspondence banks, consulting agencies or other related organizations, inquiring about the potential client's credit status. Credit inquiry contains the following parts:

1. The purpose of the letter: your requirements;
2. The reason for such requirements;
3. Expression of your expectation for an early reply.

Letter 3　Credit Inquiry

To: Bank of Montreal
From: "Wilson" <shqfoodcompany@hotmail.com>
Subject: Credit Inquiry

Dear Sirs,

You are kindly requested to provide us with the information on credit status and business operation of the firm named on the attached slip. We are to conduct business with this firm for the first time. Please include the latest financial statement, the deposit bank and account number, together with any other related credit details.

It is our usual practice to get a better understanding of our new customer's credit situation before trading. Please be convinced that all the materials provided will, of course, be kept as strictly confidential.

Your cooperation will be highly appreciated.

Yours faithfully,

Wilson

Sales Manager

After receiving the credit inquiry letter, the recipient will make a reply, providing the information inquired about and make a statement of non-liability. Such reply often includes these parts:

1. Refer to the inquiry letter and provide the preface information of the company enquired about;

2. Describe the current business situation, especially the credit standing, of the company inquired about;

3. Stress that the writer will not be held responsible for any information furnished and remind the recipient that it must be treated strictly in confidence.

Letter 4　Banker's Favorable Reply

To: "Wilson" <shqfoodcompany@hotmail.com>
From: "Amanda" <bmocomca@gmail.com>
Subject: Re Credit Inquiry

Dear Wilson,

In reply to your credit inquiry of May 6th, BMO advises that the company was originally established in 1967 by Mr. Charles D. Hinton, to conduct a business in rice and noodles. Since 1977, the firm has started to expand its business, dealing with a variety of food import.

We are glad to inform you that our business relations with the firm have hitherto been most satisfactory and they command considerable funds and an unlimited credit. Please refer to the attachment for detailed information you asked for.

Any statement here on the part of this bank or any of its officers as to the firm inquired about is given as a mere matter of opinion for which no responsibility, in any way, is to attach to this bank or any of its officers.

Yours faithfully,

Amanda

Accounting Department

Letter 5　Banker's Unfavorable Reply

To: "Wilson" <shqfoodcompany@hotmail.com>
From: "Amanda" <bmocomca@gmail.com>
Subject: Re Credit Inquiry

Dear Wilson,

This is in reply to your credit inquiry dated May 6th about the credit status of Sunny Nutritious Food Inc. BMO finds information showing that the company was originally established in 1967 by Mr. Charles D. Hinton, to conduct a business in rice and noodles. Since 1977, the firm has started to expand its business, dealing with a variety of food import.

Unfortunately, through investigation, we have found that the company is now being pressed by several creditors and its position is precarious.

This information is strictly confidential and is given without responsibility on our part.

Yours faithfully,

Amanda

Accounting Department

Having got the reply to the credit inquiry, if it is a favorable one, the businessperson will grasp the opportunity to write a letter to the potential clients, expecting to enter into business relationship. This kind of letter is almost the same as Letter 2 Request for Establishing Business Relations, except that the writer takes the initiative to provide more detailed information about the business scope and products and hopes to send more materials.

Letter 6 Establishment of Business Relations

To: Great nutritious Food Company@gmail.com
From: "Wilson" <shqfoodcompany@hotmail.com>
Subject: Establishing Business Relationship

Dear Sirs,

Through the courtesy of the Chamber of Commerce in Paris, we have obtained that you are in the market for skim milk powder, instant milk powder, infant formula milk powder and dairy by-products. We take the liberty of writing this letter in the hope of entering into business relations with you.

We have been a supplier in this line of business for many years. Our products are of superior quality and popular with our customers from all over the world. In order to give you a general idea of our products, we have enclosed a catalogue and some free samples.

Further information will be available on your request. We are awaiting your prompt reply.

Yours faithfully,

Delia Wilson

Purchasing Manager
Encl. a/s

Useful Words & Expressions

I. Widely-used Terms

1. price list	价格清单	2. illustrated catalogues	带有图片说明的目录
3. trading company	贸易公司	4. offer	报盘(报价)
5. catalogue	产品目录	6. free sample	免费样品
7. trial order	试订单	8. credit inquiry	信用查询
9. credit status	信用状况	10. financial statement	财务报表
11. deposit bank	存款银行	12. account number	银行账号
13. credit situation	征信情况	14. unlimited credit	无限制信贷
15. creditor	债权人		

II. Important Phrases

1. establish business relations	建立业务关系
2. one of the leading importers	最主要的进口商之一
3. specialize in	经营(专营)……
4. meet the standards for export	达到出口标准
5. fast-moving consumer goods	快消品
6. best price	最佳价
7. fall within	属于
8. business line	业务范围
9. take the liberty of	冒昧
10. open account with	与……建立账户往来关系
11. business operation	经营业务
12. on the attached slip	附在小便笺上
13. conduct business	开展业务
14. BMO	(加拿大)蒙特利尔银行
15. deal with	涉及
16. business relations	商业关系
17. considerable funds	拥有可观的现金
18. on the part of	就……而言

19. inquire about 查询
20. on one's part 在某人一方
21. through the courtesy of 承蒙……的介绍
22. Chamber of Commerce 商会
23. enter into business relations 建立业务关系
24. superior quality 质量上乘
25. enclose 随函附上

III. History of the Company

1. Established in 1998, Safe Healthy Quality Food Company is one of the largest experienced food trading companies in China with offices or representatives in all major cities in the country.

2. The company was originally established in 1967 by Mr. Charles D. Hinton, to conduct a business in rice and noodles. Since 1977, the firm has started to expand its business, dealing with a variety of food import.

IV. Business Scope (Self-introduction)

1. **We specialize in** canned food, such as canned fruit and vegetables.
   We are specialized in the export of arts and crafts.

2. Our assorted canned vegetables, canned fishery and canned grapes in syrup are most popular with our customers.

3. We have been a supplier in this line of business for many years.
   Our products are of superior quality and popular with our customers from all over the world.

4. Chemical products, cotton piece goods, art and craft goods, arts and crafts, handicrafts, straw and willow products, embroideries, porcelain wares, jade carvings, silk flowers, toys and gifts, fat-reducing tea, black tea, tablecloths and bath towels, imitation jewelry.

5. We deal inclusively in textiles/handle in Messrs. Haruno & Bros. Handle electronic products for export.

6. We are a state-operated corporation, handling the export of animal by-products. We are China National Textile Import and Export Corporation, with its headquarters in Beijing.

7. We are pleased to inform you that we handle a wide range of electric fans.

V. Information Sources/Channels

1. **Through the courtesy of** the Chamber of Commerce in Paris, we have obtained that you

are in the market for skim milk powder, instant milk powder, infant formula milk powder and dairy by-products.

Through the courtesy of the Paris Chamber of Commerce, we have your name as a firm who is interested in doing business with us.

Through the courtesy of Mr. White, we are given to understand that you are one of the leading importers of silk in your area.

2. **On the recommendation of** Messrs. Harvey & Co., we have learned with pleasure the name of your firm.

On the recommendation of the Bank of China, we have got to know that you import Chinese textile and cotton piece goods.

3. **We learned from** www.alibaba.com that you are a leading exporter of Chinese canned food, which falls within our business line.

4. **We learned** your name and address at the International Exhibition of Fruits and Vegetables in the *China Daily*.

We learned from the Commercial Counselor of our Embassy in New York that you deal in Machinery and Equipment.

We learned from *Times* that you are interested in gym equipment and want to order immediately.

5. **We have** your name and address from China Council for the Promotion of International Trade.

We are glad to have your name and address from *The Journal of Commerce*.

6. **Your company has been introduced to us by** Smith & Co., Ltd as prospective buyers of Chinese tablecloths. As we deal in the items, **we shall be pleased to** enter into direct business relations with you.

7. Your letter of September 8th **has been transferred to** us for attention from our Head Office in Beijing.

8. Your inquiry **has been forwarded to** us for attention from the Commercial Counselor's Office of the Chinese Embassy in Rome.

VI. Purpose of Writing

1. **We are writing this letter in the hope of** serving you with our professional experience from now on.

2. **We take the liberty of** writing this letter in the hope of opening account with you.

Unit 3 Establishing Business Relations

We take the liberty of writing this letter in the hope of entering into business relations with you.

3. **Please include** the latest financial statement, the deposit bank and account numbers, together with any other related credit details.

4. **This is in reply to** your credit inquiry dated May 6th about the credit status of Sunny Nutritious Food Inc.

In reply to your credit inquiry of May 6th,…

5. **This is to introduce** the Pacific Corporation as exporters of light industrial products having business relations with more than 70 countries worldwide.

6. **We write to introduce** ourselves as exporters of freshwater pearls with many years' experience in this particular line of business.

7. **We take the opportunity to introduce** our company as exporters dealing exclusively in leather goods.

VII. Expectations

1. Expectations for Cooperation

(1) **We are willing to** enter into business relations with you on the basis of equality and mutual benefit.

(2) As the item falls within the scope of our business, **we shall be pleased to** enter into direct business with you.

(3) **We look forward to** your close cooperation in promoting this new product.

We assure you of the best quality and competitive prices of our goods.

We assure you that we shall do our best to promote the business between us.

Your cooperation **will be highly appreciated**.

We are looking forward to our cooperation in the near future.

We would like to offer you fast-moving consumer goods with best price. Please feel free to contact us. Samples and more information are available for you anytime.

2. Expectations for Further Information

(1) **We would greatly appreciate** receiving your latest catalogue, brochure and price list. **We would also expect to** receive your free sample before placing the trial order.

(2) **We are interested in** your range of fire extinguishers and would like you to send us details of extinguishers suitable for a small office.

(3) As we are in the market for color TV sets, **we would be pleased** if you could send us your

best quotations for Panda brand color TV sets of 19 and 21 inches.

(4) **Please inform us** of the terms on which you can supply iron nails.

(5) As we are approached by our clients who are in urgent need of leather shoes for both men and women, **we would like to know** if you are able to supply shoes that meet their specific requirements.

(6) **Please refer to** the attachment for the detailed information you asked for.

3. Expectations for Early Replies

(1) **We are awaiting** your prompt reply.

(2) **We are looking forward to** your early reply.

(3) Your prompt/quick response **will be highly appreciated**.

VIII. Inquiry & Reply

1. Should your price be competitive / If your quotation is favorable, please quote your best prices.

2. Please quote us your lowest prices for personal computers.

Would you please quote us your best price CIF HK?

3. If the quality of your goods is good and the price is acceptable to us, our client will place a large order with you.

If your price can be reduced by 2%, we shall place an order for 400 cartons in our markets.

4. Upon receipt of your catalogue, we will inquire about the items that are of interest to us.

5. When quoting, please state the terms of payment and the discount you would allow for a purchase of not less than 500 dozen.

Exercises

I. Choose the best answer to complete each of the following sentences.

1. We have _____ your name and address from our partner.

   A. entered   B. obtained   C. placed   D. appreciated

2. We take this opportunity to _____ you for long-term business relations.

   A. appreciate   B. keep contact   C. approach   D. touch

3. We have specialized _____ medical instruments for more than 20 years.

   A. with   B. upon   C. for   D. in

4. We would like to _____ you the lowest price.

A. offer   B. develop   C. appeal   D. approach

5. _____ in 2015, our company specializes in the export of various kinds of toys.

     A. Establish   B. Established   C. Establishing   D. To be established

6. Samples and more information are _____ for you anytime.

     A. interested   B. available   C. useful   D. appreciated

7. We learned that you are exporting shoes, which falls _____ our business line.

     A. to   B. within   C. for   D. to

8. We are glad to introduce ourselves _____ an established importer for LED lights.

     A. on   B. of   C. as   D. with

9. Before the trial order is _____, we would like to receive your credit information.

     A. entered   B. obtained   C. confirmed   D. appreciated

10. You are kindly requested to provide us _____ your free sample.

     A. to   B. with   C. for   D. in

II. Fill in the blanks with the appropriate words or expressions.

1. _____ _____ we have found that the sample is under our standard.

2. We email you in the hope of _____ _____ business relations with you.

3. Please _____ _____ the attachment for detailed information you asked for.

4. We have been _____ _____ _____ _____ trading infant foods for 30 years.

5. Glad to _____ you that we would like to trade with you if the quotation is favorable.

III. Give the English/Chinese equivalents of the following expressions.

1. 产品目录 _____
2. 建立关系 _____
3. 专营 _____
4. 试订单 _____
5. 样品 _____
6. in the line of _____
7. owe…to… _____
8. upon receipt of _____
9. refer to _____
10. trade with _____

IV. Translate the following sentences into English/Chinese.

1. 我们的主要业务是纺织品和手工艺品。

2. 企盼与贵公司建立长期贸易关系。

3. 现附上一份最新产品目录以供参考，早复为盼。

4. We introduce ourselves as the leading exporter of infant food, which enjoys great popularity

for its exceptional quality and advanced hand craftsmanship.

5. To give you a general picture of our products, we would like to send you some free samples for reference.

6. If your offers are competitive, we are confident that we will place considerable orders with you.

V. Complete the gaps below with the appropriate words.

Letter 1

Dear Sirs,

  We have __1__ your name and email address from your websites. We are writing to __2__ if you would like to establish business relations with us.

  Established in 2008, we are a professional dealer of cases and bags in Shenzhen, China, trading in various products __3__ shopping bags, cosmetic bags, hand bags, shoulder bags, and so forth. __4__ to the standard of "good quality, and good __5__ ", our products are increasingly popular in Asian countries. For more information about our business __6__ , please __7__ to our website. We would __8__ receiving your enquiries.

  We would always be very __9__ for your early reply.

Yours faithfully,
×××

Letter 2

Dear Sirs,

  From our business partner Wilson Company, we know that you have 15 years' experience in __1__ bluetooth headsets, thus we'd like to __2__ you to __3__ long-term trade relations in the line of communication devices.

  We're __4__ in importing communication devices for a long time, __5__ a great reputation in China. As marketing research shows, there are great __6__ for your products __7__ our end. Therefore, we would be __8__ if you can provide your latest price list and free __9__ . And we will do our best to introduce your products into our market.

  Looking __10__ to your early reply.

Yours faithfully,
×××

VI. Translate the following letter into Chinese.

Dear Sirs,

We appreciate our partner for informing us of the name and address of your firm, and we understand that you are interested in expanding your wine products in the Chinese market.

We have been in the line of wine products for many years, exporting wine products to various foreign countries, including the U.K., Mexico, Canada and so on. We would like to trade with you for a long term. Please feel free to contact us, if you need any information about our company, and free samples will be available.

We shall be grateful if you will reply at an early date.

Yours faithfully,

×××

VII. Writing.

1. Suppose you (Cathy from ABC Company) met a supplier (John) last week at the trade fair in Canada, and have a keen interest in buying his products three months later. Please send him a letter including all the information below.

(1) Telling him that you are interested in his products;

(2) Requesting the latest catalogue;

(3) Requesting some free samples;

(4) Demonstrating your eagerness.

2. Imagine you (Jessica from ABC Company) received an inquiry from a potential client, Tim, asking about your newly-launched product, Model 13-9, and its quotation. And before making the specific quotation, you need to know Tim's annual order quantity. Please make a reply, including the following particulars.

(1) Expressing thanks for the inquiry;

(2) Highlighting your advantages;

(3) Expressing your hope for cooperation;

(4) Inquiring about his annual order quantity.

微课视频

扫一扫,获取本课相关微课视频。

 3.1.1　Case Study.mp4

 3.1.2　Relevant Information.mp4

 3.1.3　Writing Skills.mp4

 3.2.1　Letter 1 Seeking New Clients.mp4

 3.2.2　Letter 2 Request for Establishing Business Relations.mp4

Unit 4　Inquiries and Replies

4.1　Background Knowledge

4.1.1　Case Study

1. Case One

From the Commercial Counselor's Office of the US Embassy you have learned that Keen & Yuen Co., Ltd. has been handling lifting appliance for many years and you are in the market for such goods. What information do you hope to get? And what should you do to get the information you need?

2. Case Two

Suppose you receive the following letter, what information should be included in your letter of reply?

To: Deepseal Machinery Trading Company@hotmail.com **From:** "Mohnton Yuen" <keenyuencoltd@gmail.com> **Subject:** Establishing Business Relationship
Dear Sirs, We have seen your advertisement in *International Trade Journal* and are particularly interested in your machine tools and metal cutters. We require machines suitable for fairly heavy duty. We are the leading importer of machinery in Vietnam and have entered into business

relationships with more than 30 countries in the world. Machinery from China is very popular with our customers.

It would be appreciated if you could send us your current illustrated catalogue and a price list.

Looking forward to your prompt reply.

Yours faithfully,

Mohnton Yuen

Purchasing Manager

4.1.2 Relevant Information

In international trade, after obtaining the desired information about the companies concerned, which one wants to do business with, an inquiry letter is often sent by a buyer to inquire about the detailed information for the goods he/she wants. Business negotiations usually begin with an inquiry from an overseas buyer to a seller, inquiring about the terms or conditions of a potential sale. Sometimes, a seller can also initiate negotiations by making an inquiry to a foreign buyer to whom the seller intends to sell the products. Whoever makes an inquiry is not obligated to buy or sell. According to the commercial practice, the recipient of an inquiry should respond promptly.

1. Definition of Inquiry

Inquiry means asking. An inquiry is a request for information. It marks the beginning of the trade negotiations. In foreign trade, it is usually (not absolutely) made by the potential buyer without engagement, requesting information about the availability of certain goods. In international business, the importer may send an inquiry to an exporter, inviting a quotation and/or an offer for the goods he/she wishes to buy, or simply asking for some general information about these goods. The exporter can also send an inquiry.

2. Types of Inquiries

Generally speaking, inquiries fall into two categories: a **General Inquiry** and a **Specific**

Inquiry.

(1) **A General Inquiry** is a request for a price list, catalogue, sample or price quotation and other terms in order to get a general idea of the business scope of the exporter. This type of letter should be simple and straightforword in content.

(2) **A Specific Inquiry** is a request for goods of a particular specification. It is made when a buyer intends to conduct some business with the seller. In a Specific Inquiry, the importer specifies the products he/she needs and asks for a quotation or an offer for this item as well as some details of his/her own business such as the kind of goods handled, quantities needed, usual terms of trade and any other necessary information.

When sending a specific inquiry, many companies use a printed form for the purpose of eliminating the trouble of writing a letter.

In inquiry letters, the requirements should be clearly stated, including prices, discounts, terms of payment, shipping time, and delivery date.

An inquiry should not be addressed only to one party but also to several parties at the same time. Thus the inquirer can make a comparison between the terms of sales in the incoming offers and decide which offer is the most advantageous.

4.1.3 Writing Skills

1. Writing Skills of Inquiry Letters

When you complete an inquiry letter, it is advisable to check your letter following these skills accordingly to see whether you have made your idea clear and complete.

(1) **Frankness:** Get to the point and state how you have learned about the company and its products and what your purpose of writing the letter is. For anything uncertain, ask for a definite reply.

(2) **Clarity:** Describe your specific needs with no engagement of ordering the proposed products.

(3) **Emphasis:** Stress the importance of the information you need and politely inquire about a more detailed response.

(4) **Courtesy:** Make your letter seem as if it were written between friends and use courteous words with a pleasing tone.

2. Writing Skills of Replies to Inquiry Letters

The replies to inquiries should be prompt, courteous, and cover all the information asked for.

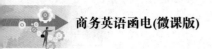

Usually, the skills below can be followed.

(1) Courtesy: Express your thanks for the inquiry received. Please your potential partners by offering as much service as needed and make the recipients feel your sincerity and heart-felt desire to conduct business with them.

(2) Completeness: Supply all the material and information inquired about, if you hope to enter into business relations with them.

(3) Clarity: Make it clear what you can do for your recipients, and if you cannot meet all of their requirements, explain why you fail to fulfill all of them. There is also such a case where you cannot satisfy the inquirer's demand at the moment. Provide the reason and assure that you will do all you can to meet his/her requirements.

(4) Concreteness: Emphasize the goods that are of interest to the buyer and your special allowances provided for him/her. If necessary, try to introduce more about your company and your products.

4.2 Sample Letters and Basic Writing Structure Analysis

4.2.1 Basic Writing Structures of Inquiry Letters

Making an inquiry should depend on your needs of general information or specific information about your potential transaction. A good inquiry usually contains the following structures.

1. State the source of the information and your understanding of the recipient;
2. Make a brief self-introduction;
3. Give your request directly;
4. Express your expectation for further contact and an early reply.

Letter 1   General Inquiry

To: DMTC@hotmail.com
From: "Mohnton Yuen" <keenyuencoltd@gmail.com>
Subject: Inquiry for Machinery Tools

Dear Sirs,

We have learned from ABC Co., Ltd., Sydney that you are a leading exporter of machinery tools in your country and you can supply all kinds of machinery equipment which falls within our

> business line.
>
> We have been handling machinery imports for many years. Now, we are very interested in importing your goods and would appreciate your illustrated catalogue and latest price list.
>
> We hope this will be a good start for our long and profitable business relations. We are looking forward to your favorable reply.
>
> Yours sincerely,
>
> Mohnton Yuen
>
> Purchasing Manager

As mentioned above, a specific inquiry is a request for goods of a certain specification. So, in a specific inquiry, the inquirer intends to conduct a deal on certain terms and conditions. Such a letter usually contains the following parts:

1. Briefly explain how you get the requested information;

2. Make a brief self-introduction and give a short introduction to your market and your ability to sell the goods to establish a good image;

3. Explain specifically why you are writing and give your specific request for the certain goods to be traded, listing the names, specifications, catalogue, price list, discount, terms of payment, delivery time, samples etc.;

4. Express your hope for further contact and an early reply.

Letter 2 Specific Inquiry

> **To:** DMTC@hotmail.com
> **From:** "Michael Smith" <smithvivemachineimportcoltd@gmail.com>
> **Subject:** Inquiry for Machinery Tools
>
> Dear Sirs,
>
> Your firm has been kindly recommended to us by Media Group, with whom we have done business for many years and have concluded many prosperous and profitable business activities.

We are Smith & Vive Machine Import Co., Ltd. in Turkey, a large importer of machinery equipment, with business connections in more than 40 countries. There is a large ready market here for our imports.

We are interested in your lathes, planers, millers and drillers and we shall be glad if you would send us a copy of your illustrated catalogue and current price list. Detailed information of CIF Antalya prices, discounts, and terms of payment will also be highly appreciated.

We are awaiting your prompt reply.

Yours sincerely,

Michael Smith

Purchasing Manager

4.2.2 Basic Writing Structures of Favorable Replies to Inquiry Letters

A good reply to an inquiry should be prompt, courteous, objective and comprehensive, and contain all the information required. The seller should try to promote the sale by giving an accurate description of commodities and other attractive terms and conditions. It usually contains the information as below:

1. Express thanks for the inquiry, restating the date and the request of the inquiry;

2. Provide all the details/materials asked for and also offer additional information/materials not included in the inquiry, if necessary;

3. Speak highly of your own company/product;

4. Express thanks/sincerity for doing business with the recipient.

Letter 3   A Reply to General Inquiry

To: "Mohnton Yuen" <keenyuencoltd@gmail.com>
From: "Hunter Chen" <deepsealmachinerytradingcompany@hotmail.com>
Subject: Your Inquiry for Machinery Tools

Unit 4 Inquiries and Replies

Dear Mohnton,

Thank you for your inquiry of June 2nd and for your interest in our commodities. We are enclosing some copies of our illustrated catalogue and a price list giving the details you asked for. Enclosed please also find our other products which may arouse your interest.

We trust you will agree that our products and prices appeal to the most selective buyers. And we also offer a proper discount according to the quantity ordered.

Thank you again for your interest in our products. We are looking forward to your order and you may be assured that it will receive our prompt and careful attention.

Yours truly,

Hunter Chen

Export Manager

Letter 4 A Reply to Specific Inquiry

To: "Michael Smith" <smithvivemachineimportcoltd@gmail.com>
From: "Hunter Chen" <deepsealmachinerytradingcompany@hotmail.com>
Subject: Your Inquiry for Machinery Tools

Dear Michael,

We are pleased to learn from your inquiry of June 8th that our lathes, planers, millers and drillers are of your interest.

We are in a position to supply you the goods in large quantities from our wide selections of different models. You can get a 2.5% quantity discount, if you place an order for over US$100,000. We usually accept confirmed and irrevocable L/C payable by draft at sight.

We have enclosed our illustrated catalogue and the latest price list, quoting prices CIF C2.5%

Antalya. We are sure you will find a fast sale for our products at your end as they have sold well throughout other countries.

Any orders you may place with us will have our prompt attention. We are awaiting your early reply.

Sincerely yours,

Hunter Chen

4.2.3 Basic Writing Structures of Unfavorable Replies to Inquiry Letters

Sometimes the inquiry gets a partial refusal, not a complete acceptance, due to some reason or another. The structure of such an unfavorable reply shares some similarities with the favorable one, but also some differences, as listed below:

1. Express your thanks for the inquiry, your willingness to do what you can as requested, and your regret for inability to accept the entire request;

2. Give your reason for refusal, and try to offer a substitute or additional information, if necessary;

3. Express the expectation of doing business with the recipient.

Letter 5　Refusal to General Inquiry: Declining a Buyer's Request

To: "Michael Smith" <smithvivemachineimportcoltd@gmail.com>
From: "Hunter Chen" <deepsealmachinerytradingcompany@hotmail.com>
Subject: Re: Your Inquiry for Machinery Tools

Dear Michael Smith,

Thank you for your inquiry dated 20th May. We are always pleased to hear from a valued customer. However, I regret to say that we cannot provide the technical information you requested regarding our products, due to the fact that most of our competitors also keep such information private and confidential.

I sincerely hope that this does not cause inconvenience to you. If there is any other way in which we can help you, please do not hesitate to contact us again.

Thanks again for your inquiry and looking forward to your cooperation.

Truly yours,

Hunter Chen

Letter 6　Refusal to Specific Inquiry: Refusing to Send the Full Range of Samples

To: "Michael Smith" <smithvivemachineimportcoltd@gmail.com>
From: "Hunter Chen" <deepsealmachinerytradingcompany@hotmail.com>
Subject: Re: Your Inquiry for Machinery Tools

Dear Michael Smith,

Thank you for your inquiry dated 16th July. We are pleased to hear that you are interested in our products.

In compliance with your requirement, we have airmailed you the samples of a rivet gun, a manual screwdriver, a jig and a linear cutter. However, I regret to say that we cannot send you the full range of samples, such as an electric screwdriver, a pneumatic screwdriver and a laser-cutter. Our company has a cost control policy for providing free samples. You are the first one to receive so many free samples.

When you receive the samples, you can be assured that our products are of standard parts with high-quality workmanship and only the best quality materials are used. They will appeal to the most discriminating buyers.

Attached please find our latest price list, which quotes prices CIF C2.5% Antalya of our products. For detailed information and full illustrations of our products, please refer to our online catalogue at www.deepsealmachinerytrading.com. We look forward to receiving your order soon.

Yours faithfully,

Hunter Chen

Useful Words & Expressions

I. Widely-used Terms

    1. terms of payment   支付条款

    2. confirmed and irrevocable L/C payable by draft at sight   保兑的、不可撤销信用证，凭即期汇票支付

    3. full range of samples   全套样品

II. Important Phrases

    1. enter into business relationship   建立业务关系

    2. do business   从事商业活动

    3. ready market   现成的市场

    4. illustrated catalogue   图文目录

    5. selective buyer   挑剔的买家

    6. quantity ordered   订购数量

    7. prompt and careful attention   迅速周到安排(处理)

    8. be in a position to do   有能力做某事

    9. place an order for sth.(with sb.)   (向某人)订购……商品

    10. Please do not hesitate to contact us.   请随时与我们联系。

    11. in compliance with   按照……

    12. cost control policy   成本控制政策

    13. appeal to   吸引

    14. discriminating buyer   挑剔的买家

III. Business Scope (Self-introduction)

    1. **We are the leading importer of machinery** in Vietnam and have entered into business relationships with more than 30 countries in the world.

    2. **We have been handling** machinery imports for many years.

Unit 4 Inquiries and Replies

3. We are Smith & Vive Machine Import Co., Ltd. in Turkey, a large importer of machinery equipment, with business connections in more than 40 countries.

IV. Information Sources/Channels

1. **We have seen your advertisement in** *International Trade Journal* and are particularly interested in your machine tools and metal cutters.

2. **We have learned from** ABC Co., Ltd., Sydney **that** you are a leading exporter of machinery tools in your country and you can supply all kinds of machinery equipment which falls within our business line.

3. **Your firm has been kindly recommended to us by** Media Group, with whom we have done business for many years and have concluded many prosperous and profitable business activities.

V. Inquiring About Specific Information on Products/Prices

1. Now, **we are very interested in** importing your goods and would appreciate your illustrated catalogue and latest price list.

2. **We are interested in** your lathes, planers, millers and drillers and we shall be glad if you would send us a copy of your illustrated catalogue and current price list.

3. **Detailed information of** CIF Antalya prices, discounts, and terms of payment **will also be highly appreciated**.

4. **It would be greatly to your interest to** make a trial of these goods.

May we expect a trial order from you while prices are greatly in your favor?

5. As there is a heavy demand at this time of the year for heaters, you will have to allow at least 6 weeks for delivery.

6. **We require** the machine suitable for fairly heavy duty.

VI. Reply

1. Expressing Thanks

(1) **Thank you for your inquiry** of June 2nd and for your interest in our commodities.

Thank you for your inquiry dated 20th May. We are always pleased to hear from a valued customer.

Thank you for your inquiry dated 16th July. We are pleased to hear that you are interested in our products.

We thank you for your inquiry of February 2nd and are pleased to tell you we are in good connections with the best manufacturers in the country.

Thank you for your letter of January 14th. Enclosed please find our summer catalogue and price list giving details of CFR Sydney prices.

(2) **We are pleased to learn from your inquiry of** June 8th that our lathes, planers, millers and drillers are of your interest.

We are glad to learn from your inquiry of February 8th that you are interested in our ladies' blouses. As requested, our catalogue and price list are enclosed together with details of our sales conditions.

We were pleased to receive your inquiry of March 10th for our Portable Mixer Model PM-222.

We are pleased to quote you the best price.

(3) **We have much pleasure in** enclosing a quotation sheet for our products and trust that their high quality will induce you to place a trial order.

In accordance with the request of… at the Guangzhou Fair, **we have pleasure in** sending you herewith the samples and a price list for...

We take pleasure in making you an offer as required by you some time ago, subject to our final confirmation.

(4) **Thank you again for** your interest in our products.

Thanks again for your inquiry and looking forward to your cooperation.

2. Favorable Replies to Inquiry Letters

Providing Details/Materials

(1) We are **enclosing** some copies of our illustrated catalogue and a price list giving the details you asked for.

Enclosed please also find our other products which may arouse your interest.

We have **enclosed** our illustrated catalogue and the latest price list, quoting prices CIF C2.5% Antalya.

(2) You can get a 2.5% quantity **discount**, if you **place an order for** over US$100,000.

(3) We usually accept confirmed and irrevocable L/C payable by draft at sight.

(4) Attached please find our latest price list, which quotes prices CIF C2.5% Antalya of our products. For detailed information and full illustrations of our products, please refer to our online catalogue at www.deepsealmachinerytrading.com.

(5) We can supply most items from stock and will have no trouble in meeting your delivery

needs.

We can allow you a special discount of 2% on the prices quoted for a quantity of 50 or more.

(6) We would like to draw your attention to the trade and quantity discounts offered in our publicity brochure on pp.16-24, which may be of particular interest to you.

Advantages of the Company/Products

(1) **We trust you will** agree that our products and prices appeal to the most selective buyers. And we also offer a proper discount according to the quantity ordered.

(2) **We are sure you will** find a fast sale for our products at your end as they have sold well throughout other countries.

(3) When you receive the samples, you **can be assured that** our products are of standard parts with high-quality workmanship and only the best quality materials are used.

(4) Our products will **appeal to** the most discriminating buyers.

(5) Machinery from China **is** very **popular with** our customers.

3. Unfavorable Replies to Inquiry Letters

(1) However, **I regret to say that we cannot** provide the technical information you requested regarding our products, **due to** the fact that most of our competitors also keep such information private and confidential.

I regret to say that we cannot send you the full range of samples, such as an electric screwdriver, a pneumatic screwdriver and a laser-cutter.

(2) **We regret that it is impossible to** accept your counter-offer, even to meet you halfway; the price of raw material has increased by 20%, and we shall shortly be issuing an updated price list.

(3) **Although we are** eager to establish business relations with you, **we regret that it is impossible** for us to grant the reduction you requested, as we have already reduced our prices to the lowest possible point after reviewing our cost calculations.

VII. Expectations

1. Expectations for Further Contact

(1) **It would be appreciated if** you could send us your current illustrated catalogue and a price list.

(2) **We hope this will be a good start for** our long and profitable business relations.

(3) **We are looking forward to** your order and you may be assured that it will receive our prompt and careful attention.

(4) Any orders you may place with us will have our prompt attention.

(5) If there is any other way in which we can help you, **please do not hesitate to** contact us again.

2. Expectations for Early Reply

(1) **Looking forward to** your prompt reply.

　　We are looking forward to your favorable reply.

　　We look forward to receiving your order soon.

(2) We **are awaiting** your prompt reply.

　　We are awaiting your early reply.

Exercises

I. Choose the best answer to complete each of the following sentences.

1. We can provide all kinds of plastic products _____ buyers worldwide.
   A. for　　　　B. by　　　　C. at　　　　D. with

2. We have been _____ hiking shoes import and export for many years.
   A. issuing　　B. inquiring　　C. handling　　D. fulfilling

3. We would _____ your sending us illustrated catalogues and lowest quotation.
   A. inquire　　B. convince　　C. appreciate　　D. confirm

4. This trial order will be good for our long and _____ business relations.
   A. accessible　　B. profitable　　C. unfavorable　　D. considerable

5. Your firm has been kindly _____ to us by Gates Group.
   A. followed　　B. informed　　C. encountered　　D. recommended

6. We have _____ many prosperous business activities with clients from South America.
   A. concluded　　B. appealed　　C. enclosed　　D. quoted

7. We found a large _____ market here at our end for your products.
   A. ready　　B. enclosed　　C. against　　D. respective

8. _____ please also find our other products which may arouse your interest.
   A. Enclosure　　B. Enclosing　　C. Enclose　　D. Enclosed

9. A 5%-10% discount will be _____ according to the quantity you ordered.
   A. granted　　B. inquired　　C. enclosed　　D. quoted

10. We are _____ a position to supply you the goods in large quantity.
    A. for　　B. by　　C. in　　D. with

Unit 4 Inquiries and Replies

II. Fill in the blanks with the appropriate words or expressions.

1. Please _____ us your best price CIF Seattle.

2. We are pleased to learn that our goods are _____ your interest.

3. Our illustrated catalogue has been _____ for your reference.

4. Our products will surely find a fast sale _____ _____ _____.

5. You may be assured that our products will _____ your clients' needs.

6. As your requirement, we have sent you the free _____ you asked for.

III. Give the English/Chinese equivalents of the following expressions.

1. 询盘 _____   2. 报价_____

3. 报价单 _____   4. 下订单 _____

5. 样品 _____   6. 特殊折扣 _____

7. attachment _____   8. in a position _____

9. for one's reference _____   10. illustrated catalogue ____

IV. Translate the following sentences into English/Chinese.

1. 我们相信我们的新产品在欧洲将很畅销。

2. 如果你方价格和条件满足我方要求，我们愿意开展合作。

3. 感谢贵司的报价，请问是否能够提供现货？

4. We are offering you the instruments which cannot be obtained elsewhere at such a low price.

5. It would be appreciated if you could send us your current illustrated catalogue and a price list.

6. As requested, we are now enclosing a competitive price list to you.

V. Complete the gaps below with the appropriate words.

Letter 1

Dear Mr. Tian,

   I would like to __1__ an inquiry on items as __2__:

   a. 5,000 sets TM-42 lamps

   b. 3,000 sets TM-23 LED Lamps

   Could you please __3__ CIF Miami price before July 10th? It is __4__ if you can inform us whether you can make the __5__ of the above within four weeks after __6__ of the order.

  I look forward to your __7__ soon, as we are __8__ an order from one of our close contacts. We hope this will also lead to more __9__ orders.

Yours sincerely,
× × ×

Letter 2

Dear Vivi,

  Thank you very much for your inquiry __1__ May 23rd about our mountain bikes. As __2__, we have emailed you our illustrated catalogues and price lists.

  As to the __3__ of payment, it's a practice to trade __4__ the basis of sight L/C.

  Our products have enjoyed __5__ in the world market for their excellent quality and high performance for years. We are __6__ that our products will no doubt help you __7__ your market.

  For more information, please __8__ to our website.

  We are __9__ your early reply.

Yours sincerely,
× × ×

VI. Translate the following letter into Chinese.

Dear Sirs,

  From one of our partners in Europe, we know that you are a dealer of boots in which we also trade. It is found that there is a steady demand at our end.

  It would be appreciated if you could send us your latest price list with detailed specifications. It would also be helpful if you could supply some free samples for our customers' reference.

  As winter is coming, an early reply will be appreciated.

Yours faithfully,
× × ×

Unit 4　Inquiries and Replies

VII. Writing.

Letter 1

Imagine you are Jane from an American shoes import company named SOFT, and you get to know a shoes supplier in Brazil by searching the Internet. Now you are writing to George to make an inquiry.

1. Telling him how you got his name and address;

2. Mentioning the products you are interested in;

3. Asking for the latest catalogue and price;

4. Inquiring about the payment terms and delivery details.

Letter 2

You (Rock) have received an inquiry from a new buyer (King) about your LED light model 276, and you are invited to make a quotation. You are required to write a letter to him including the information below.

Write to reply to your client's inquiry about your products.

1. Expressing thanks for the inquiry;

2. Making a quotation by listing the details;

3. Expressing your hope for a trial order.

 微课视频

扫一扫，获取本课相关微课视频。

4.1.1　Case Study.mp4　　4.1.2　Relevant Information.mp4　　4.1.3　Writing Skills.mp4

4.2.1　Letter 1 General Inquiry.mp4　　4.2.1　Letter 2 Specific Inquiry.mp4　　4.2.2　Letter 4 A Reply to Specific Inquiry.mp4

Unit 5 Offers and Counter-offers

5.1 Background Knowledge

5.1.1 Case Study

1. Case One

Suppose you are the salesperson of an electronic products export company. You received an inquiry from an overseas company, asking for information about your goods and trade terms and conditions. Now your manager requires you to make an offer in reply. What would you write?

2. Case Two

Suppose you are Loran, receiving the following letter. What is the purpose of the writer? What will you write in your reply?

| **To:** "Loran Evans" <carljoinc@gmail.com> |
| **From:** "Scott" <liangshengelectroniccompany@hotmail.com> |
| **Subject:** Your Inquiry of July 16th |
| Dear Loran,

Thank you for your inquiry of July 16th saying that you are interested in our range of electronic appliances.

We are in a position to supply you from our wide selection of electronic appliances suitable for households, hotels or offices. Enclosed, you will find our quotation sheet quoting prices CIF |

C2% Antwerp. We are sure there will be a ready sale for our products at your end.

Looking forward to your early response. We assure you that any orders you place with us will receive our prompt attention.

Yours sincerely,

Scott Wood

Sales Manager

5.1.2　Relevant Information

In international trade, after receiving an inquiry letter, the other party will give you a favorable or unfavorable reply. In the case of a favorable reply, the price and the other trade terms of the commodity to be traded will be offered. This is the second stage of business negotiation: offer. A reply to an offer will generate a counter-offer, or an acceptance. However, in the case of an unfavorable reply, establishing business contact of this time is almost impossible.

In international trade practice, finalizing a business often involves a series of counter-offers and counter-counter-offers. In business negotiations, a process of offers, counter-offers and counter-counter-offers is needed until a transaction is concluded or called off.

1. Definition of Offer

An offer is actually a proposal of certain trade terms or an expression of a willingness to sell or to buy certain goods according to the terms and conditions proposed. An offer is usually made by the seller, known as a "selling offer", and sometimes it can also be made by the buyer, known as a "buying offer" or "bid". The one who makes the offer is called the offeror. The one who receives the offer is called the offeree. An offer of goods is usually made either through advertisements, circulars, and letters or in reply to inquiries. This is the second step in business negotiation.

2. Types of Offers

In practice, there are two popular types of offers. One is a "firm offer" and the other is a "non-firm offer".

(1) Firm Offer

A firm offer is a definite promise to sell certain goods at the stated prices, usually within a stated period of time. The terms stated in a firm offer are binding on the seller if they are accepted by the buyer within its validity. In a firm offer, an exact description of the goods, the time of shipment and the mode of payment should be included. Once it is unconditionally accepted by the offeree within its validity, it cannot be revoked or amended and is binding on both parties.

Normally, a firm offer has such expressions as "We are making you the following under-mentioned offer, subject to your acceptance before/by/not later than…", "We make this offer for your acceptance/confirmation within… days", "This offer is subject to your reply arriving at us by/on or before/not later than…, Beijing time", "This offer is/keeps firm/good/open for… days only," etc.

(2) Non-firm Offer

Unlike a firm offer, a non-firm offer is not binding upon the seller. A non-firm offer, also known as a soft-firm offer, is an offer without engagement. In other words, a non-firm offer can be withdrawn or changed by the offeror at will. A non-firm offer has no period of validity. In most cases, the contents of it are not clear and definite. It usually contains certain reservation clauses, such as "We offer without engagement…", "The offer is subject to our final confirmation", "The offer is subject to prior sale", "This offer is subject to change/alteration/variation without (previous) notice", etc.

(3) Counter-offer

A counter-offer is made when a prospective buyer finds any terms and conditions in the offer unacceptable. Therefore, in a counter-offer, the original offeree partly accepts or totally refuses the offer but puts forward some new proposals for the trade; thus, a counter-offer is actually a new offer from the original offeree. It has dual roles: first, a counter-offer is a rejection to the original offer; second, a counter-offer is a new offer. After receiving the counter-offer, the offeror may make concessions if he/she thinks the suggestion acceptable; otherwise he/she may bring up some new terms and conditions, which is called counter-counter-offer. This process may go round and round before the two parties come to terms of the transaction. Silence or inactivity during the validity period of the offer constitutes a decline.

5.1.3 Writing Skills

1. Writing Skills of Firm Offer Letters

Based on the features and purpose of a firm offer, when writing a letter to make a firm offer, the writer should be aware of the following three points:

(1) Conciseness: The offer must be written clearly to indicate that it is firm.

(2) Clearness and Completeness: The offer must be clear, definite, complete and final, and it must indicate all the main terms and conditions for the transaction.

(3) Validity: The offer must contain the expression of the validity.

2. Writing Skills of Counter-offer

The counter-offer plays an even more important role in determining the final terms and conditions for the trade. So, when making a counter-offer, the offeror should bear in his/her mind the following skills:

(1) Self-knowledge: Know yourself fairly well

In a counter-offer, the writer must bear in his/her mind which issues are the most important and what concessions he/she is willing to make. He/she also has to determine what a "must" is and what is not.

(2) Frankness: Be frank and straightforward

Be honest with the seller about your interest in the products. Being straightforward about the goods you are interested in will not only save your time, but also bring a profitable transaction, without revealing all your bargaining strategies. Furthermore, it facilitates you to suggest a willingness to pay at the price you can accept and also signals that you are serious, which finally helps you get the transaction to your expectation.

(3) Bargaining: Demand concessions

Research shows that if you immediately accept the offer at the very beginning, the offeror will likely to be filled with regret. Remember that the transaction you are asking for should be your profitable one and the other party's satisfactory one. So even if the first offer is close to your ideal, you should still demand concessions. Thus you will not only achieve a more advantageous outcome for yourself, but also increase the other party's satisfaction.

5.2 Sample Letters and Basic Writing Structure Analysis

5.2.1 Basic Writing Structures of Offer Letters

An offer, firm or non-firm, is of great importance to determine the terms and conditions for the trade, so the writer of such a letter should be careful to make sure the letter includes the following points:

1. An expression of thanks for the inquiry and making a confirmation of the date of the inquiry, if any;

2. Indicate all the information requested, such as details of prices, discounts, terms of payment, delivery or shipping date, as well as what the prices cover (e.g., freight, insurance, etc.);

3. Give additional information concerning the business;

4. If it is a firm offer, state the period of validity;

5. Include one or two lines encouraging the customer to place an order and assuring them of your best service.

Letter 1   Firm Offer Letter

To: "Caspar"<kevincameraequipmentinc@gmail.com>
From: "Hank Liang" <guangmeiphotographicequipmentcoltd@hotmail.com>
Subject: Offer of Photographic Equipment

Dear Caspar,

Thank you very much for your inquiry dated July 18th inquiring about our photographic equipment.

We are pleased to make you a firm offer, subject to your reply here by 5 p.m. Beijing time, July 22nd, as follows:

Product Name: Multi-Function Tripods

Price: USD 40 per set CIF C2% Arica

Payment: confirmed, irrevocable letter of credit, to be opened 30 days before the time of shipment, payable by draft at sight

Packing: 1 set per inner box, 6 boxes per carton

Shipment: Not later than September 30th

Minimum Quantity: 500 sets

The stock is running short. If the offer satisfies you, only an early order can catch the chance. Please click the attachment for more information about our products, which may be of your interest.

We look forward to your early order.

Yours sincerely,

Hank Liang

Sales Manager

Letter 2 Non-firm Offer Letter

To: "Jacob"<ronaldcameraequipmentinc@gmail.com>
From: "Hank Liang" <guangmeicoltd@hotmail.com>
Subject: Offer of Photographic Equipment

Dear Jacob,

Thank you for your letter dated July 16th. As requested, we are airmailing you one catalogue and two samples for our multi-functional transformers and universal chargers to help you make your selections.

In order to start a transaction between us, we take pleasure in making you a special offer airmailed under separate cover, subject to our final confirmation.

We trust the price and the quality will be acceptable to you and await with keen interest your trial order.

Yours sincerely,

Hank Liang

Sales Manager

5.2.2 Basic Writing Structures of Counter-offer Letters

As discussed above, a counter-offer means partly accepting or totally refusing the offer but putting forward some new proposals for the potential business; thus, the writer of a counter-offer letter should make sure it contains the following points:

1. Show your appreciation for the offer received;
2. Express regret for inability to accept the offer and give your reasons;
3. Propose your own terms and conditions in the counter-offer;
4. Express your desire, hoping that your counter-offer will be accepted.

Letter 3　Counter-offer Letter

To: "Todd"<gabrielgreattradecoltd@gmail.com> **From:** "Spencer Huang" <hengxinelectronicgroupcorporation@hotmail.com> **Subject:** Your Offer for Bluetooth Keyboard & Touch Pen
Dear Todd, Thank you for your letter of July 20th, offering us the subject goods. In reply, we regret to say that our clients find your price to be on the high side. Information indicates that the said articles, supplied in other countries, have been sold here at about 5% lower than that of yours. The quality of your products is slightly superior, but the difference in price should, in no case, be so significant. To facilitate the trade, we propose a 4% price reduction in our counter-offer, subject to your reply here by July 26th. As the market is of keen competition, we recommend your immediate consideration and acceptance of our offer. Yours sincerely, Spencer Huang Sales Manager

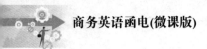

5.2.3　Basic Writing Structures of Replies to Counter-offer Letters

When receiving a counter-offer, the offeree usually replies transmitting the following information:

1. Accept the counter-offer and conduct business, or;

2. Decline the counter-offer and maintain the original offer, or;

3. Conditionally accept the counter-offer and make a further counter-offer.

Letter 4　A Reply to Counter-offer Letter

To: "Mason" <emeraldmodernofficetradecoltd@gmail.com>

From: "Spencer Huang" <hengxinelectronicgroupcorporation@hotmail.com>

Subject: Your Counter-offer for Card Reader & Memory Card

Dear Mason,

Thank you for your counter-offer of July 20th, but we find your price is too low.

For the card reader, we can conduct business only on the basis of USD 12 per piece CIF Augusta. The 16GB USB flash drive is priced at USD 13 per piece, the 32GB USB drive at USD 20 each, and the 64GB at USD 36 each. We usually accept payment by cash with order (CWO) for orders from new clients. Shipment can be made within one week after the order is confirmed.

Should the above proposal be accepted, we assure you of our best products and services at any time.

Yours sincerely,

Spencer Huang

Sales Manager

Useful Words & Expressions

I. Widely-used Terms

1. quotation sheet   报价单   2. firm offer   实盘
3. product name   品名   4. time of shipment   交货日期
5. minimum quantity   最低起订量   6. counter offer   还盘(还价)
7. cash with order (CWO) 随单付现支付方式

II. Important Phrases

1. ready sale   畅销
2. subject to   以……为准
3. the stock is running short   库存不足
4. under separate cover   在另函中
5. keen interest   很感兴趣
6. offering sb. the subject goods   向某人提出特定货物的报价
7. price on the high side   价格偏高
8. the said articles   上述商品
9. keen competition   竞争激烈

III. Expressing Thanks and Making a Confirmation

1. **Thank you for your inquiry of** July 16th saying that you are interested in our range of electronic appliances.

2. **Thank you very much for** your inquiry dated July 18th inquiring about our photographic equipment.

3. Thank you for your letter dated July 16th.

Thank you for your letter of July 20th, offering us the subject goods.

4. Thank you for your counter-offer of July 20th, but we find your price is too low.

IV. Providing Detailed Information/Reasons

Offer Letters

1. **We are pleased to make you a firm offer,** subject to your reply here by 5 p.m. Beijing time, July 22nd, as follows:

Product Name: Multi-Function Tripods

Price: USD 40 per set CIF C2% Arica

Payment: confirmed, irrevocable letter of credit, to be opened 30 days before the time of shipment, payable by draft at sight

Packing: 1 set per inner box, 6 boxes per carton

Shipment: Not later than September 30th

Minimum Quantity: 500 sets

2. Please click the attachment for more information about our products, which may be of your interest.

3. As requested, we are airmailing you one catalogue and two samples for our multi-functional transformers and universal chargers to help you make your selections.

4. In order to start a transaction between us, **we take pleasure in making you a special offer** airmailed under separate cover, subject to our final confirmation.

5. **We are in a position to** supply you from our wide selection of electronic appliances suitable for households, hotels or offices.

6. **Enclosed,** you will find our quotation sheet quoting prices CIF C2% Antwerp.

Counter-offer Letters

1. In reply, **we regret to say that** our clients find your price to be on the high side. Information indicates that the said articles, supplied in other countries, have been sold here at about 5% lower than that of yours.

2. The quality of your products is slightly superior, but the difference in price should, in no case, be so singnificant.

3. **To facilitate the trade**, we propose a 4% price reduction in our counter-offer, subject to your reply here by July 26th.

4. We **desire to call your attention to** our special offer. You will readily understand that this offer is good only for acceptance reaching us before the end of… In view of the heavy demand for this line, we advise you to send orders as soon as possible.

Reply to Counter-offer Letters

1. For the card reader, we can conduct business only on the basis of USD 12 per piece CIF Augusta. The 16GB USB flash drive is priced at USD 13 per piece, the 32GB USB drive at USD 20 each, and the 64GB at USD 36 each.

2. We usually **accept payment by cash with order** (CWO) for orders from new clients. Shipment can be made within one week after the order is confirmed.

3. We do not see any advantage in your **quotations**, and would like to know if you have any

better options to offer.

4. Your competitors are offering considerably lower prices, and unless you can **reduce your quotations,** we shall have to buy the products elsewhere.

5. We thank you for your offer, but we are buying at lower prices. Are these the best prices you can offer?

V. Suggestions/Expectations for Further Contact

1. **Looking forward to** your early response. We assure you that any orders you place with us will receive our prompt attention.

　　We look forward to your early order.

2. The stock is running short. If the offer satisfies you, only an early order can catch the chance.

3. **We trust** the price and the quality will be acceptable to you and **await with keen interest** your trial order.

4. As the market is of keen competition, we **recommend** your immediate consideration and acceptance of our offer.

5. Should the above proposal be accepted, **we assure you** of our best products and services at any time.

6. **We are sure** there will be a ready sale for our products at your end.

Exercises

I. Choose the best answer to complete each of the following sentences.

1. Special discount is made when the _____ order quantity is larger than 2,000 sets.

　　A. repeat　　　　B. maximum　　　　C. first　　　　D. minimum

2. Agreement can be reached only _____ the basis of US$32 per set CIF New York.

　　A. on　　　　B. of　　　　C. as　　　　D. with

3. Shipment can be made _____ one week after the order confirmed.

　　A. within　　　　B. to　　　　C. for　　　　D. when

4. _____ the competition is keen, an immediate reply to the offer will be appreciative.

　　A. On　　　　B. Of　　　　C. As　　　　D. With

5. We are making an offer to you subject _____ your reply here by July 21st.

　　A. within　　　　B. to　　　　C. for　　　　D. on

6. We trust the price and the quality we offered will be _____ to you.

   A. available   B. acceptable   C. useful   D. appreciated

7. To start a practical transaction, we take pleasure _____ making you a special offer.

   A. to   B. in   C. for   D. by

8. The _____ is for more information about our newly-developed products.

   A. discount   B. offer   C. attachment   D. quotation

9. We are pleased to make you a firm offer as _____.

   A. follow   B. following   C. follows   D. followed

10. So sorry to inform you that your price is found _____ the high side.

   A. to   B. on   C. for   D. in

II. Fill in the blanks with the appropriate words or expressions.

1. We hope you can agree _____ our offer.

2. Orders you may place _____ us will have our prompt attention.

3. We are prepared to _____ you a special discount of 5%.

4. There will surely be a ready sale for your products _____ our end.

5. We are able to supply you _____ our stock of electronic appliances.

6. We counter offer a 4% price _____ for we will place a considerable order.

III. Give the English/Chinese equivalents of the following expressions.

1. 减价 _____   2. 有效期 _____

3. 以……为准 _____   4. 最小订单量 _____

5. 议付 _____   6. 利润空间 _____

7. out of stock _____   8. special allowance _____

9. firm offer _____   10. final confirmation _____

IV. Translate the following sentences into English/Chinese.

1. 根据你方要求，现给你方报价，此报价以我方最终确认为准。

2. 年订单量少于 50 000 美元，将无法获得折扣。

3. 很抱歉我们不能够接受你的发盘。

4. This offer is open until your reply reaches us by August 12th, 2023(our time).

5. Owing to the declining market, we hope you can agree to our offer soon.

6. If concession can be made on your price, say 8% discount, we would like to close the deal.

Unit 5 Offers and Counter-offers

V. Complete the gaps below with the appropriate words.

Letter 1

Dear John,

   Thank you for your inquiry of 20th December and we are __1__ our offer for tablecloth.

   We have made a good selection of patterns __2__ fine quality, attractive designs, and the __3__ prices, which will convince you that these materials are really of good value. __4__, there is a heavy __5__ for our goods from house furnishers at your end, which is reported by marketing researches, but __6__ that we receive your order __7__ two weeks, we will give our priority to it for prompt __8__.

   Your early reply will be __9__.

                                                        Yours faithfully,
                                                        ×××

Letter 2

Dear Sirs,

   We appreciate your inquiry of 21st April and the sample.

   After the inspection of the sample, we may assure you that we are __1__ a position to produce the similar products in design and quality as __2__.

   For an __3__ need of 50,000 units, we offer you as __4__:

   Price: USD $ 0.5 per unit CIF Sydney

   Packing: waterproof bags for inner packing, crates for outer packing

   __5__: by irrevocable L/C at sight

   Shipment: within 60 days after __6__ of your order

   We can assure you that this price is the __7__ based on the above quantity. You may __8__ to our price list and catalogue.

                                                        Yours faithfully,
                                                        ×××

   __9__: a copy of price list and catalogue

VI. Translate the following letter into Chinese.

Dear Jack,

   Thank you for your inquiry of 20th July regarding your interest in our bedspreads.

   We are able to supply products in various designs and colors from stock. We are delighted to offer you as below:

Price: USD 12 per yard CFR Los Angeles

Payment: by irrevocable L/C at 30 days sight

Shipment: 4 weeks after order confirmed

Validity: your reply here by August 2nd our time

Looking forward to receiving your order soon.

Sincerely yours,

Tom

VII. Writing.

1. Imagine you (Simona) are a dealer of T-shirt in China, and you have received an inquiry from an Indian client (Nina) about 50,000 dozen men's T-shirts. Write to make a firm offer by including the information below.

(1) Expressing thanks and referring to the inquiry;

(2) Listing out the details of the offer;

(3) Setting the validity;

(4) Persuading an early order by showing some market research information.

2. Suppose your supplier (Martin) has made you an offer for 300 sets of medical equipment, but you (Johnson) don't agree on the price and discount. Write to counter-offer.

(1) Expressing thanks for the offer;

(2) Pointing out the exact item(s) you want to change and giving the alternatives;

(3) Supporting your counter-offer with some market research information;

(4) Showing the hope and value of closing the deal.

 微课视频

扫一扫，获取本课相关微课视频。

5.1.1　Case Study.mp4

5.1.2　Relevant Information.mp4

5.1.3　Writing Skills.mp4

5.2.1　Letter 1 Firm Offer Letter.mp4

5.2.1　Letter 2 Non-firm Offer Letter.mp4

5.2.2　Letter 3 Counter-offer Letter.mp4

Unit 6　Orders and Acknowledgements

6.1　Background Knowledge

6.1.1　Case Study

1. Case One

Suppose that you have received an offer and find the garments offered suitable for your market. The terms and conditions are acceptable to you, so you decide to write a letter, placing an order for the garments in the hope of fulfilling all your requirements. What information should you include in your letter?

2. Case Two

Suppose you are the secretary in the purchasing department of the company. Your manager, Neil, receives the following letter and asks you to deal with it. What will you do before writing a letter in reply? What will you write in your reply?

To: "Neil Wang" <fashionleaderapparelcompany@hotmail.com>
From: "Gloria Ford" <fordjohninc@gmail.com>
Subject: Our Order No. TS1709

Dear Neil,

Thank you for your offer. We are very much interested in your T-shirts illustrated in Catalogue No. TS-368.

We are glad to place an order with you for your cotton T-shirt as follows:

Commodity: 200 dozen for TS-86, at US$150/dozen

300 dozen for TS-87, at US$180/dozen

300 dozen for TS-88, at US$200/dozen

Price terms: CIF Messina

Delivery time: before the end of October, 2023

Shipment: by sea, partial shipment and transshipment are PROHIBITED

Payment: by irrevocable sight L/C

We are looking forward to your early reply.

Yours faithfully,

Gloria Ford

Purchasing Manager

6.1.2 Relevant Information

1. Definition of an Order

After rounds of negotiation, if the buyer accepts the seller's offer, the buyer may choose to send out an order letter to inform his/her decision of placing an order. An order may result from the buyer's acceptance or confirmation of a firm offer made by the seller or from the seller's acceptance or confirmation of a counter-offer from the buyer. So, an order is a formal request for a certain quantity of specific goods at a certain price to be fulfilled within a certain period of time.

2. Main Contents of an Order

An order, especially when it is an initial order, must adhere to the important principles of clarity and accuracy so as to avoid misunderstandings and troubles in the future. Therefore, an order usually includes such details as:

(1) Description of the goods, such as specification, size, quantity, quality and article number (if any);

(2) Price and mode of payment: unit prices and the total amount; terms of payment and the

time of payment;

(3) Packing and marking requirements;

(4) Shipping or forwarding instructions: mode of transportation, time of shipment, port of destination, transshipment and partial shipment;

(5) Other necessary details.

3. Forms of an Order

An order may take the form of a letter, a telegram, a telex message, a fax, an e-mail message or a printed order form. Most orders today are placed using standardized order forms, purchase forms, and requisition forms, and are processed through standardized procedures. Additionally, a letter will usually go together with these forms of order.

6.1.3 Writing Skills

1. Writing Skills of Order Letters

When writing an order letter, the writer may express the hope of being given prompt and careful attention to the order besides the details mentioned above. So, the writer, also the buyer, should follow such skills as:

(1) Courtesy: An order means a real beginning of mutual cooperation between the two parties. To facilitate the success of the order and to further the deals, the writer should express his/her pleasure in the business opportunity in the letter.

(2) Clarity and completeness: Write a concise but complete letter, telling the seller what you want directly without any ambiguity, listing all your requirements without leaving out anything necessary.

(3) Unreservedness: An order can be regarded as acceptance or confirmation of an offer, signifying the two parties have agreed upon the main terms and conditions of the transaction. So, when writing such a letter, the writer should keep in mind that the order will be restricted by these terms and conditions, not allowing further negotiations.

2. Writing Skills of Reply to Order Letters

When receiving an order, the seller should reply without any delay to indicate his/her acceptance or refusal according to the real situation. A deal is concluded only when the buyer and the seller are willing to enter into a contract in accordance with the terms and conditions agreed upon. In such reply letters, the following writing skills are strongly recommended to observe:

(1) **Courtesy:** Whether to accept or to decline an order, in the reply, the seller should express gratitude at the very beginning of the letter, and show sincerity for future and further cooperation.

(2) **Hopefulness:** For an acceptance, express your expectation for more future business; for a refusal, leave room for future cooperation and make your refusal relative and non-absolute by generalizing the terms so that the buyer does not think the refusal only applies to him/her, and inform the buyer you are willing to enter into business relations with him/her once you can fulfill his/her order.

(3) **Consideration:** Reply immediately upon receiving the letter, indicating your acceptance gratefully or your refusal regretfully, and promise to provide the best service to the other party's future orders.

6.2　Sample Letters and Basic Writing Structure Analysis

6.2.1　Basic Writing Structures of Order Letters

As discussed above, an order is a direction from the buyer to the seller for the purchase of some specific goods on some certain terms and conditions. When writing a letter to place an order, the buyer should make sure that the letter is arranged in such a way as follows:

1. Express thanks for the offer and state the decision to place an order, showing interest in certain items;

2. Provide full details of the order and the main terms and conditions, indicating the name of commodity, specification, article number, quantity, price terms, types of packaging, shipment, and all other relevant information that will enable the seller to fulfill the order without any further questions;

3. Close the letter by expressing willingness to cooperate or suggesting future business dealings;

4. Expect for the earliest reply.

Letter 1　An Order Letter

To: "Glen" <fashioncolorclothingtradingcoltd@hotmail.com>
From: "Marvin" <marvinlanegarmentsinc@gmail.com>
Subject: Our Order No. G5678 for 2,000 Cotton T-shirts

Dear Glen,

Thank you for your offer of July 6th. We are interested in your T-shirts and are glad to place an order with you on the terms agreed upon between us.

Details of the order are as follows:

Specification: equal assortment of black and white with S to XL Size as illustrated in Catalogue No. 26

Price: USD 22 per shirt FOB Shanghai

Payment: payable by irrevocable confirmed sight L/C

Shipment: not later than August 10th

Packing: each in a polybag, every ten in a paper box, 20 boxes in a carton

Since this is the first order, we will pay special attention to the quality. If this order turns out to be satisfactory, there will be a flow of other orders.

Looking forward to receiving our order early.

Sincerely yours,

Marvin Bush

Chief Purchasing Officer

A repeat order has nothing special in nature. What appears in an initial order may also be contained in a repeat order. But because of the previous dealing, the buyer is familiar with the seller's usual practices and the details of the products. Thus, a repeat order may be simpler, with many details omitted.

The following points are usually contained in a repeat order:

1. Express satisfaction with the fulfillment of previous orders;
2. Inform the seller of the buyer's intention to place a repeat order;
3. State the requirements, indicating any needed improvements or changes in business conditions;
4. Close the letter with confident expectations for the order.

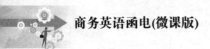

Letter 2　A Repeat Order Letter

To: "Glen" <fashioncolorclothingtradingcoltd@hotmail.com>
From: "Marvin" <marvinlanegarmentsinc@gmail.com>
Subject: Our Order No. G5682 for 2,000 Cotton T-shirts

Dear Glen,

We have received the 2,000 dozen T-shirts and find the quality satisfactory. The T-shirts have received favorable reactions from our customers.

We are glad to inform you that there is a great demand in our market for your products. We wish to place with you a repeat order No. G5682 for 2,000 dozen of the same specification, color and sizes.

We'll open the relevant L/C upon receipt of your Sales Confirmation and hope you will make delivery at an early date.

Yours faithfully,

Marvin Bush

Chief Buyer

6.2.2　Basic Writing Structures of Replies to Order Letters

After receiving an order, the seller can either fulfill or decline it. Once an order is accepted by the seller, a transaction is concluded and a contract or confirmation will be signed between both parties.

In a letter of confirming an order, the seller should develop it in such a way to:

1. Acknowledge the order with thanks;

2. Restate the important information, such as the contents of the order, price, shipment, payment, packing, etc.;

3. Assure the buyer of prompt and careful execution of the order;

4. Add a few favorable comments on the goods ordered, express your desire for future orders and draw attention to other products likely to be of interest, if possible.

Letter 3   Accepting an Order

To: "Marvin" <marvinlanegarmentsinc@gmail.com>
From: "Glen Huang" <fashioncolorclothingtradingcoltd@hotmail.com>
Subject: Your Order No. G5678 for 2,000 Cotton T-shirts

Dear Marvin,

Thank you for your order of July 10th for 2,000 cotton T-shirts at USD 22 per shirt FOB Shanghai, payable by irrevocable confirmed sight L/C, with shipment not later than August 10th.

We are now enclosing our S/C covering the Order No. G5678 in duplicate. Please countersign and return one copy to us for our records. Upon receipt of your relevant L/C, we will get the goods ready and arrange shipment as requested. You will be kept fully informed of the progress.

We have confidence that you will be completely satisfied with our products when you receive them. For your reference to the wide range of our products, we are attaching a copy of our latest catalogue in the hope of furthering business between us and marking the beginning of a happy and friendly working relationship.

Sincerely yours,

Glen Huang

Sales Manager

An order can't always be accepted. Such reasons as follows will result in a refusal:
1. The goods required are not available;
2. Prices and specifications have been changed;
3. The buyers and the sellers cannot agree on some terms of the business;
4. The buyer's credit is not in good standing;

5. The manufacturer simply does not produce the goods ordered, etc.

If turning down an order, the seller should include the following information in his/her letter:

1. Express appreciation for pleasure in receiving the order and show regret for inability to be helpful;

2. Give the detailed reasons for turning down the order;

3. Offer suitable substitutes and make counter-offers to show the sincerity of cooperation and persuade the buyer to enter into an agreement;

4. Express expectation for future business relations.

Letter 4　Turning down an Order

To: "Marvin" <marvinlanegarmentsinc@gmail.com>
From: "Glen Huang" <fashioncolorclothingtradingcoltd@hotmail.com>
Subject: Your Order No. G5678 for 2,000 Cotton T-shirts

Dear Marvin,

Thank you for your order of July 10th for 2,000 cotton T-shirts, indicating shipment to be made not later than August 10th.

However, due to heavy demand for our products in this season, we are fully committed and we regret for our inability to entertain any fresh orders now, so we cannot meet your date of delivery.

But, we will keep your order before us. Once our supply is replenished, we will contact you by e-mail immediately. Or you may find some substitutes in our latest catalogue attached. All your orders will obtain our immediate attention.

Thank you for your consideration. We hope to entertain your next order as required.

Sincerely yours,

Glen Huang

Sales Manager

Unit 6 Orders and Acknowledgements

Useful Words & Expressions

I. Widely-used Terms

1. commodity   商品
2. price terms   价格条款
3. delivery time   交货时间
4. shipment   装运
5. payment   支付
6. partial shipment   部分装运
7. transshipment   转运
8. packing   包装
9. repeat order   续订单、追加订单
10. relevant L/C   相关的信用证
11. sales confirmation 销售确认书
12. S/C   销售合同
13. in duplicate   一式两份

II. Important Phrases

1. flow of orders   持续不断的订单
2. receive favorable reactions from our customers 收到客户的良好反应
3. make delivery at an early date   尽早交货
4. for one's reference   供某人参考
5. wide range of…   各种各样
6. further business   促进业务合作
7. inability to entertain any fresh orders   无法接受任何新订单
8. keep one's order before sb.   优先考虑某人的订单
9. supply is replenished   储备得到补充
10. entertain your next order   接受你方下一个订单

III. Expressing Thanks and Satisfaction

1. **Thank you for your offer of** July 6th.

Thank you for your offer. We are very much interested in your T-shirts illustrated in Catalogue No. TS-368.

2. **Thank you for your order of** July 10th for 2,000 cotton T-shirts, indicating shipment to be made not later than August 10th.

3. **Thank you for your** consideration.

4. **Thanks for your letter of** November 2nd with catalogue and price list.

5. **We are interested in** your T-shirts and are glad to place an order with you on the terms

agreed upon between us.

6. We have received the 2,000 dozen T-shirts and find the quality **satisfactory**.

7. The T-shirts have received **favorable reactions** from our customers.

8. **We are glad to inform you that** there is a great demand in our market for your products.

IV. Providing Detailed information of the Order

1. **Details of the order are as follows:**

Specification: equal assortment of black and white with S to XL Size as illustrated in Catalogue No. 26

Price: USD 22 per shirt FOB Shanghai

Payment: payable by irrevocable confirmed sight L/C

Shipment: not later than August 10th

Packing: each in a polybag, every ten in a paper box, 20 boxes in a carton

2. We are glad to **place an order** with you for your cotton T-shirt as follows:

Commodity: 200 dozen for TS-86, at US$150/dozen

300 dozen for TS-87, at US$180/dozen

300 dozen for TS-88, at US$200/dozen

Price terms: CIF Messina

Delivery time: before the end of October, 2023

Shipment: by sea, partial shipment and transshipment are PROHIBITED

Payment: by irrevocable sight L/C

3. Since this is the first order, we will pay special attention to the quality. If this order turns out to be satisfactory, there will be a flow of other orders.

4. We wish to **place with you a repeat order** No. G5682 for 2,000 dozen of the same specification, color and sizes.

We shall **place a large order** with you provided the quantity of the goods and the shipping period meet our requirements.

If this first order is executed to our satisfaction, we shall **place further orders** with you. The material supplied must be absolutely waterproof, and we **place our order** subject to this guarantee.

5. **We are pleased to place the following orders** with you if you can guarantee shipment from Shanghai to Singapore by October 9th.

We are pleased to place an order with you for 100,000 sets of MP3 players.

Your samples of Red Leaf Brand Health Tea have received favorable reactions from our

Unit 6 Orders and Acknowledgements

clients, and **we are pleased to enclose our order** for 400 cartons.

6. **We order** 100 units of Italian furniture No. TS-11 at $300 per unit FOB Genoa. If this order is acceptable, please let us know by SWIFT.

7. **We enclosed a trial order**. If the quality is up to our expectations, we shall send further orders in the near future. Your prompt attention to this order will be appreciated.

We enclosed our order, but must point out that the falling market here will leave us little or no margin of profit. We must ask you for a better price for future supplies.

8. **We** have selected four qualities and **take pleasure in enclosing our order** sheet No. 26.

We have the pleasure of sending you an order for 1,000 dozen umbrellas, at US$45 per dozen CIF New York, based on your catalogue No. 51 of July 1st. We trust the prices mentioned therein are still in force.

V. Accepting an Order

1. We are now enclosing our S/C covering the Order No. G5678 in duplicate. Please countersign and return one copy to us for our records.

2. Upon receipt of your relevant L/C, we will get the goods ready and arrange shipment as requested.

3. You will be kept fully informed of the progress.

4. We require full payment at the time of placing an order, and do not accept deposits or offer payment plans.

VI. Reasons/Suggestions for Turning down an Order

1. **Due to** heavy demand of our products in this season, we are **fully committed** and **we regret for** our inability to entertain any fresh orders now, so we cannot meet your date of delivery.

2. We will keep your order before us. Once our supply is replenished, we will contact you by e-mail immediately.

3. You may find some substitutes in our latest catalogue attached. All your orders will obtain our **immediate attention**.

4. **We regret that we cannot** at present entertain/fill any new orders for… owing to heavy orders.

5. **We are sorry to** ask you to reduce 1,000 pieces from Order No. 123 due to economic depression (wrong calculation).

6. **We are sorry we cannot** accept your request to increase the quantity because we have

already completed the production, and it would be difficult to prepare the materials for the increased small quantity.

VII. Expectations for Further Contact

1. **Looking forward to** receiving our order early.

We are looking forward to your early reply.

2. We'll **open the relevant L/C upon** receipt of your **Sales Confirmation** and hope you will make delivery at an early date.

3. **We have confidence** that you will be completely satisfied with our products when you receive them.

4. **For your reference to** the wide range of our products, we are attaching a copy of our latest catalogue in the hope of furthering business between us and marking the beginning of a happy and friendly working relationship.

5. **We hope to** entertain your next order as required.

Exercises

I. Choose the best answer to complete each of the following sentences.

1. We would like to appreciate your offer _____ 2,000 pairs of hiking shoes _____ US$115 per pair CIF Los Angeles.

    A. for, by   B. for, at   C. against, at   D. for, with

2. Enclosure is the order with all the terms and conditions _____ which we agreed.

    A. at   B. on   C. to   D. with

3. The _____ L/C will be faxed to you as soon as it is issued.

    A. covered   B. covering   C. cover   D. covers

4. Would you please inform us _____ your annual order quantity?

    A. to   B. with   C. of   D. by

5. We are pleased to order the _____ items.

    A. follows   B. following   C. as follows   D. as following

6. We will appreciate if you can give our order prompt _____.

    A. payment   B. priority   C. attention   D. stock

7. If there is anything I can do to speed up the order, call me _____ our new number.

    A. to   B. with   C. against   D. by

8. We are working hard to _____ your order.

   A. meet   B. encounter   C. fulfill   D. cancel

9. We would like to make an apology _____ the delay in handling your order.

   A. to   B. of   C. against   D. for

10. Thanks for your email which _____ the order you made last week.

    A. confirm   B. confirmed   C. inform   D. informed

11. The discount granted is only based _____ the minimum order quantity of 2,000.

    A. with   B. on   C. against   D. for

12. Look forward to _____ your order soon.

    A. receive   B. receiving   C. receives   D. received

13. We appreciate your order, but we regret _____ to disappoint you.

    A. to have   B. to having   C. having   D. have

14. _____ please find the Sales Contract.

    A. Enclosure   B. Enclosing   C. Enclosed   D. Being enclosed

15. We regret to tell you that there is no stock _____ for your order.

    A. available   B. advisable   C. considerable   D. preferable

II. Fill in the blanks with the appropriate words or expressions.

1. Please keep us _____ of the process of our order No. 6235.

2. Would you like to order only 1,000 sets _____ no discount?

3. We are sending you our Sales Contract No. 175 _____ duplicate.

4. Would you please speed up opening the L/C once the order is _____?

5. We would like to _____ an order _____ you _____ the following items.

6. We are trying to find another supplier to _____ your outstanding orders.

7. Any discount will be _____ based on the minimum quantity over 10,000 units.

III. Give the English/Chinese equivalents of the following expressions.

1. 附件 _____

2. 最低起订量 _____

3. 处理订单 _____

4. 一式两份 _____

5. 及时发货 _____

6. 确认订单 _____

7. fulfill the order _____

8. inform sb. of sth. _____

9. sales contract _____

10. purchase order _____

IV. Translate the following sentences into English/Chinese.

1. 现以每件150美元CIF纽约价向贵司订购NC156 T恤2 000件。

2. 订单装船日期不应晚于2024年5月1日。

3. 感谢贵司的订单，但由于订单数量小于最小订单量2 000件，我方不能给予折扣。

4. We are now confirming our agreement on the purchase of the goods as follows.

5. Both your quality and prices are found to be satisfactory, and we are pleased to order the following items from you.

6. As the goods ordered last week are urgently needed, please note that it is important to make punctual shipment within the validity of the L/C.

V. Complete the gaps below with the appropriate words.

Letter 1

Dear Ms. Lee,

    We have __1__ your offer of 30th July __2__ 1,200 dozen of down jackets. We are __3__ an order with you, and could you please keep us __4__ of the whole process, because our clients need it urgently.

    We are __5__ the covering L/C through the Bank of China, and will send it to you once it is __6__.

    Since the winter is coming, it is appreciated if you make a __7__ shipment before October 10th. We firmly believe that your products will __8__ a high reputation at our end.

    We hope this will also lead to more __9__ orders.

                                       Yours sincerely,

                                                   ×××

Letter 2

Dear Mr. Liu,

    Thank you for your e-mail of March 23rd in which you __1__ the order form of 500 pairs of our hiking boots GS102.

    We __2__ your order, but it is difficult for us to __3__ you a 5% discount which is based on a __4__ quantity of 2,000 pairs.

    We would like you to __5__ your order before June 1st, so that we have enough time to __6__ your order before the delivery date of July 10th. Please __7__ that as we have a number of __8__ orders to fulfill, it would be appreciated if your L/C could reach us a week after the contract is __9__.

Unit 6 Orders and Acknowledgements

> Looking forward to receiving your reply soon.
>
> > Yours sincerely,
> > ×××

VI. Translate the following letter into Chinese.

> Dear Ms. Xu,
>
> We appreciate your Order No. 532 for 1,500 dozen shoes, and are pleased to inform you that the goods can be supplied from stock.
>
> Regarding the method of payment, we would like you to open an irrevocable L/C for a sum of US$18,000 with a validity period until August 10th. Upon receipt of confirmation of the L/C, we will get your order ready for shipment.
>
> We hope that the goods will reach you in good time and that we may have further orders from you.
>
> > Yours faithfully,
> > ×××

VII. Writing.

1. You (Prince) have received the offer and sample for T-shirt L2351 from your supplier (Tim) and found the offer acceptable, so you decided to place an order for 1,000 dozen T-shirts L2351. Besides, to ensure you can take advantage of the selling season, you have to persuade Tim to make a timely shipment. Write to your supplier with the following given particulars:

   (1) Confirm and express thanks for the sample;

   (2) Place an order for 1,000 dozen T-shirts L2351;

   (3) Ask for a timely delivery.

2. Your client (Tony) has placed an order with you for 1,000 dozen down jackets GM1365. You (Lucas) are pleased to confirm the order and have to ask for the timely L/C. Write to your client with the following given particulars:

   (1) Express thanks for the order;

   (2) Restate the important items;

   (3) Ask for the timely opening of the L/C.

微课视频

扫一扫，获取本课相关微课视频。

6.1.1　Case Study.mp4　　6.1.2　Relevant Information.mp4　　6.1.3　Writing Skills.mp4

6.2.1　Letter 1 An Order Letter.mp4　　6.2.2　Letter 3 Accepting an Order.mp4　　6.2.2　Letter 4 Turning down an Order.mp4

Unit 7　Packing

7.1　Background Knowledge

7.1.1　Case Study

1. Case One

Suppose you are the purchase manager of an international export company dealing in glassware and chinaware. You place an initial order and want to send the exporter your packing requirements. What will you write in your letter of packing instructions?

2. Case Two

You are Morin, the sales manager, receiving the following letter from a valued client. What lesson do you learn from the case mentioned in this letter? In your reply, what will you write?

To: "Morin" <fortmachinerytradinginc@gmail.com>
From: "Walton" <parkergchardwaretradingcoltd@hotmail.com>
Subject: Our Order No. WL1705026
Dear Morin, Thanks for the timely shipment of our order No. WL1705026. But we regret to inform you that of the 30 cases of machine parts, five were seriously damaged. Considering the long and friendly relations between us, we refrain from lodging a claim this time. But we feel it necessary to stress the importance of trustworthy packing for your future

deliveries to us.

Machine parts are susceptible to shock and must be wrapped in soft materials and firmly packed in seaworthy cases to avoid movement inside the cases. The bright metal parts should be protected from dampness and rust in transit by a coating of anti-rust grease.

We trust that you can meet the above requirements and thank you in advance for your cooperation.

Yours faithfully,

Walton

Sales Manager

7.1.2　Relevant Information

In foreign trade, goods will have to travel a long distance before reaching the clients abroad. Therefore, packing occupies a very important position in foreign trade. Appropriate packing avoids or reduces losses and disputes, earning you not only profits but also clients. Packing involves the selection of materials, structures, styles, ways of decoration, design, etc. It helps protect goods, reduce warehousing costs, freight and damages, and also reflects the achievements of a country's science, technology, art and culture.

The goods should be packed in a way according to the importer's instructions or the trade customs without violating the importing country's regulations on outer packing material, length and weight, or going against the importing country's social customs and national preference for inner packing colors and designs, etc.

1. The Major Packing Methods

Generally, there are two main packing methods: outer packing and inner packing.

(1) Outer Packing

Outer packing, also named transportation packing or large/giant packing, is used mainly to keep the goods safe and sound, facilitate the transporting, loading, unloading, storage, identification and numbering. Outer packing is often standardized, well suited for long distance transportation, and offers protection from damage and theft.

(2) Inner Packing

Inner packing, usually small and exquisite, looking attractive and appealing, is designed for the promotion of sales, suitable for window display and facilitating marketing, therefore, also called sales packing or small packing. When inner packing contains only one unit of the goods in each package, it is also referred to as individual packing.

2. The Main Packing Containers and Ways of Packing

Different packing containers are used for different goods. As usual, the packing is arranged in the following ways:

(1) Bags, sacks, cartons, cases, boxes and crates are used for solid goods in general;

(2) Drums, barrels, casks and kegs are used for liquid goods in large quantities;

(3) Cans or tins are used for liquid goods and food in small quantities;

(4) Bales are used for soft goods like cotton and wool;

(5) Carboys are used for chemicals.

3. Points for Attention to the Ways and Styles of Packing

When negotiating the nature of packing, the two parties should take the following points into consideration:

(1) The goods: The value, the nature, the size and weight are all important factors to help determine the choice of packing. Goods of great value should go with high-quality packing. Fragile goods should be packed with great care to avoid shock and any rough handling. The ease of handling and stowage limits the size of packing.

(2) The transportation: Modes of transportation, the distance, and variations in temperature during the course of the transit all affect the ways of packing.

(3) The customs or statutory requirements: Packing should be in compliance with the customs or statutory requirements of the importing country.

Besides, preference of the importing country, insurance acceptance conditions and marketing considerations also affect the packing.

4. Marks

To facilitate the identification of goods, the outer packing must be marked clearly with identifying symbols and numbers which should be the same as indicated in the commercial invoice, the bill of lading and other shipping documents. Marks can be generally divided into three categories: shipping mark (main mark), indicative and warning marks, and supplementary (or additional) marks. The last two are also called side marks.

(1) Shipping Mark

Shipping marks are often stenciled, serving as identification of the consignment to which they belong. It is usually a symbol consisting of the name or initials of the consignee or shipper, destination and piece number, serial number, contract number or order number, etc.

(2) Indicative and Warning Mark

Indicative and warning marks give handling instructions in words or by internationally recognized symbols. Indicative marks often have such expressions as "Do Not Drop", "This Side Up", "Keep Dry", "Handle with Care", etc. Warning marks are used to warn the person concerned against the danger of the goods that are flammable, explosive, poisonous, radioactive, and so on.

(3) Supplementary (or Additional) Mark

Supplementary (or additional) marks are used to indicate the country of origin, dimensions and weight on every package as required in some countries' foreign trade regulations.

7.1.3　Writing Skills

In foreign trade, letters concerning packing usually involve packing proposals, packing instructions or requirements, packing confirmations, informing details of packing, etc.

1. Writing Skills of Letters Concerning Packing Instructions

In order to facilitate handling and protecting the goods, the buyer usually gives the seller packing instructions, especially for the initial order. In a letter of packing instructions, the following skills are generally employed:

(1) Courtesy: Open the letter by expressing thanks for the transaction and give instructions with a friendly tone. If necessary, give brief reasons for your instructions. End the letter by expressing your expectation for an early reply and wishes for further business.

(2) Completeness: Offer detailed descriptions of the packing requirements, including inner packing, outer packing, packing materials, packing quantities, packing styles and even the design. If marks are required, try to give sufficient indications.

(3) Conciseness: Just focus on your packing instructions, and end the letter when you complete this task.

2. Writing Skills of Letters Concerning Packing Improvement

In practice, if the packing is found to be not so good or if some damage or loss is caused by the packing and/or the marks, the packing and/or marks must be changed and improved. Letters concerning this topic should follow these skills:

(1) Directness: Go straight to the point, referring to the problem and give requirements for improving or changing the future packing and/or marks without concealing anything.

(2) Consideration: Express your thanks for the cooperation and your regret for the trouble of changing the packing and/or marks. Describe the new packing and/or requirements in great detail and give the reasons.

(3) Definiteness: Avoid ambiguous words and expressions. Show your attitude towards the improvement of packing clearly and definitely and your strong expectation for the recipient's approval.

3. Writing Skills of Letters Concerning Informing the Details of Packing

(1) Conciseness: Open the letter by directly pointing out the matter or problem of packing under discussion.

(2) Completeness and Consideration: Explain the packing and shipping arrangements in great detail. In case the writer wants the reader to change the packing method or to accept the new packing method, detailed reasons should be provided.

(3) Courtesy: End the letter by asking for cooperation or expressing wishes for an early reply.

7.2 Sample Letters and Basic Writing Structure Analysis

7.2.1 Basic Writing Structures of Letters Concerning Packing Proposal

In foreign trade, the buyer usually gives packing proposals to the seller, especially for the first order between the two parties. In such a letter, the buyer should contain the following contents:

1. Refer to the transaction, mentioning the order No. and/or the contract No.;
2. Specify the packing requirements;
3. Indicate the expectations.

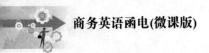

Letter 1 Buyer's Packing Proposal

To: "Karl" <kingboxgarmentcoltd@gmail.com>
From: "Neil" <elegantapparelinc@hotmail.com>
Subject: Packing Proposal for S/C No. SW1708

Dear Karl,

We would like to refer to our order for 500 dozen of KB sweaters and your sales confirmation No. SW1708.

Particular care should be taken about the packing of the goods to be delivered in the first order. It is the usual practice here that one sweater is packed in an inner polybag, and an outer paper box, 10 to a carton and 10 cartons to a strong seaworthy wooden case, lined with a waterproof sheet. There will be a flow of orders if this initial order proves to be satisfactory.

We trust this order will be the first of a series of deals between us. We are looking forward to your reply for confirmation.

Yours sincerely,

Neil Brown

Overseas Purchasing Manager

7.2.2 Basic Writing Structures of Letters Concerning Packing Instructions

A letter about packing instructions is something like the one concerning packing requirements, but the former is more specific and detailed, in a definitely affirmative tone. When the buyers try to give the packing instructions, they should:

1. Express thanks for the previous letter and refer to the matter of packing;
2. Give the inner packing and outer packing instructions;
3. State the ways to make the marks;
4. Indicate expectations and hope for an early confirmation.

Letter 2 Buyer's Packing Instructions

To: "Ford" <fuzhouuniontradingcoltd@aliyun.com>
From: "Evan" <ellenshshoesinc@hotmail.com>
Subject: S/C No. SF-1708

Dear Ford,

Thank you for your letter dated August 2nd, enclosing the above sales contract in duplicate for us to countersign. However, after going through the contract, we find that the packing clause in it is not clear enough. In order to eliminate possible future troubles, we would like to make clear our packing requirements as follows:

The leather boots under the captioned contract should be packed in paper boxes, each pair to a box, 20 boxes in an export cardboard and 10 cardboards in a wooden box. On the outer packing, please mark our initials ESSI in a diamond, under which the port of destination, London and our order number 1708091 should be stenciled. In addition, indicative marks like KEEP DRY, USE NO HOOKS, etc., should be indicated.

Your special attention to the packing will be greatly appreciated. We look forward to your confirmation and shipping advice.

Yours sincerely,

Evan Lysacek

Overseas Purchasing Manager

7.2.3 Basic Writing Structures of Letters Informing the Details of Packing

After confirming packing requirements, the seller completes packing and will often inform the buyer of the detailed information about packing. The letter always has these parts:
 1. Express thanks for the order together with the information concerning shipment arrangement;
 2. Specify the detailed packing information;
 3. Indicate the expectation for more deals.

Letter 3 Informing the Details of Packing

To: "Debbie" <easefashiontradinginc@hotmail.com>
From: "Judy" <zhenyuanelectroniccoltd@aliyun.com>
Subject: Your Order No. EF7082

Dear Debbie,

Thank you for your order No. EF7082 for our smart phone touch screens and replacement parts. The consignment is to be dispatched today as contracted, and should arrive within three weeks.

The touch screens, individually wrapped in waterproof foam sheets, are surrounded by soft padding and packed into small tin boxes, each measuring 16cm×8cm×5cm. The replacement parts have been put separately into bubble plastic bags and packed in cartons. The tin boxes and cartons are packed into non-returnable wooden cases with lifting hooks provided at four points.

We have the confidence that the consignment will reach you safe and sound, and the goods will turn out to be satisfactory. We are awaiting more orders from you.

Yours sincerely,

Judy Cheng

Overseas Sales Manager

7.2.4 Basic Writing Structures of Letters for Improving Future Packing

In foreign trade, though the two parties have accepted the packing method, regarding it as safe and reliable, in transit sometimes such packing is found to be inappropriate, because such packing is vulnerable to causing damage to or loss of the goods. In such a case, to avoid further loss in future dealings, the buyer will write to the seller, requiring him/her to improve the packing. Letters for this purpose generally contain the following information:

1. Express thanks for the shipment of the goods and direct the problem at the same time;
2. Give a brief reason;
3. State the new packing requirements;
4. Expect for acceptance.

Letter 4   Improving Future Packing

To: "Walt" <kinfumetaltradingcoltd@aliyun.com>
From: "Burt" <goldenjoyshardwareinc@hotmail.com>
Subject: Your S/C No. KF-7060

Dear Walt,

Thank you for your timely shipment of the goods under our order No. GK1706 and your S/C No. KF-7060. Unfortunately, upon arrival, we found that of the 100 cartons of screws, ten cartons were delivered, damaged, and the contents had spilled, leading to some losses.

We agree that the loss caused is not your fault. However, in order to avoid any similar incidents, we feel it necessary to clarify the concrete stipulations for our future dealings.

We require that the future packing be in wooden cases of 20 kilos net each, with each wooden case containing 40 cardboard packs of 500 grams net. Each wooden case should be furnished with a handle.

Please let us know whether these specifications can be met by you and whether they will lead to an increase in your prices.

Yours sincerely,

Burt Brown

Overseas Purchasing Manager

Useful Words & Expressions

I. Widely-used Terms

1. carton	纸箱	2. seaworthy(wooden) cases	适于海运的(木)箱
3. outer paper box	外纸盒	4. trustworthy packing	可靠的包装
5. lined with	内衬	6. sales contract	销售合同
7. initial order	首次订单	8. packing clause	包装条款
9. countersign	会签	10. export cardboard	出口纸箱
11. lifting hooks	吊钩	12. indicative marks	指示性标记
13. diamond	菱形图案	14. port of destination	目的港
15. waterproof	防水	16. captioned contract	标题项下的合同

II. Important Phrases

1. lodge a claim　　　　　　　　　提出投诉
2. packed in..., and..., to...　　　　(商品)用……包装，(若干包装)入……
3. go through　　　　　　　　　　检查
4. safe and sound　　　　　　　　安然无恙
5. future dealings　　　　　　　　今后的交易

III. Expressing Thanks

1. **Thanks for** the timely shipment of our order No. WL1705026.

2. **Thank you for your letter** dated August 2nd, enclosing the above sales contract in duplicate for us to countersign.

3. **Thank you for your order** No. EF7082 for our smartphone touch screens and replacement parts.

4. **Thank you for your timely shipment of** the goods under our order No. GK1706 and your S/C No. KF-7060.

IV. Specifying the Packing Requirements/Instructions (Buyer)

1. Machine parts **are susceptible to** shock and must be **wrapped** in soft materials and firmly **packed in** seaworthy cases to avoid movement inside the cases.

2. The bright metal parts **should be protected from dampness and rust in transit** by a

coating of anti-rust grease.

3. **Particular care should be taken about the packing of the goods** to be delivered in the first order.

4. **It is the usual practice here that** one sweater is packed in an inner polybag, and an outer paper box, 10 to a carton and 10 cartons to a strong seaworthy wooden case, lined with a waterproof sheet.

5. In order to **eliminate possible future troubles**, we would like to **make clear** our packing requirements as follows.

6. The leather boots under the captioned contract should be **packed in** paper boxes, each pair to a box, 20 boxes in an export cardboard and 10 cardboards in a wooden box.

7. On the outer packing, please mark our initials ESSI in a diamond, under which the port of destination, London, and our order number 1708091 should be stenciled.

8. In addition, **indicative marks** like KEEP DRY, USE NO HOOKS, etc., should be indicated.

9. The 0.5 liter tins of paint will be supplied in strong cardboard cartons, each containing 48 tins, with a gross weight of 50 kg.

10. All export bicycles are **wrapped in** strong waterproof material at the port and packed in pairs in lightweight crates.

The fragile goods should be **wrapped in** soft material and firmly packed in cardboard boxes.

11. **A special crate with** reinforced bottom **will be needed for** the transport of such a large machine, and both padding and bolting down will be essential.

12. **We object to packing in** cartons unless the flaps are glued down and the cartons secured by metal bands.

13. **Great care must be given to packing** as any damage in transit would result in a great loss.

14. Please **limit the weight** of each carton to 10 kg and use metal straps for all cartons in stacks of 4.

15. Please cut vent-holes in the cases to minimize **condensation**.

16. Please note that the packing we require is 6pcs in an inner box and 6 inner boxes in an export carton.

17. **We require that the future packing** be in wooden cases of 20 kilos net each, with each wooden case containing 40 cardboard packs of 500 grams net.

18. **Please see to it that the packing is** strong enough to withstand rough handling.

19. **The packing must be** seaworthy.

20. Please **take necessary precautions, so that** the packing can protect the goods from dampness or rain/leaking/pilferage.

It is imperative that you **take special precautions to prevent** a recurrence of this type of damage.

V. Reply to Buyer's Packing Requirements/Instructions

Specifying the Detailed Packing Information (Seller)

1. The touch screens, individually **wrapped in** waterproof foam sheets, are surrounded by soft padding and **packed into** small tin boxes, each measuring 16cm×8cm×5cm.

2. The replacement parts have been **put** separately **into** bubble plastic bags and packed in cartons. The tin boxes and cartons are **packed into** non-returnable wooden cases with lifting hooks provided at four points.

We will **pack** the material **in** bales of approximately 2 meters in length and 3 meters in girth.

The protective canvas will be provided with lifting ears to facilitate lifting.

We **pack** our shirts **in** plastic-lined, waterproof cartons, reinforced with metal straps.

3. **We have the confidence that** the consignment will reach you safe and sound, and the goods will turn out to be satisfactory.

4. **Our usual packing for** dyed poplin **is** in bales lined with waterproof paper, each containing 500 yards of a single color.

Our usual packing for tea has proven successful for a long time in many export shipments.

5. **Careful consideration has been taken into packing**. We have improved it, so as to avoid damage to the goods.

6. We provide both 10-foot and 20-foot containers. They open at both ends, thus facilitating loading and unloading.

7. For goods liable to be spoiled by damp or water, our containers **have the advantage of** being watertight and airtight.

8. **This new packaging for our products appeals** strongly to consumers.

This new packaging for our products facilitates marketing in supermarkets and retail outlets.

9. The appearance of the package contributes greatly to the sales of our products.

10. The packaging of this article features a novel design and a variety of styles.

Conditions for Accepting Buyer's Requirements

1. **We are ready to accept** orders to be packed or packaged with your own materials.

2. Your way of packing takes time.

3. **We'll accept your requirements** for packing, but the design must be in our hand at least 18 days before the time of shipment.

4. We'll accept your requirement for packing with your materials, but the materials must be in our hand at least 30 days before the time of shipment.

5. I'm afraid we'll have to charge more for the designated packing as it calls for extra labor and expenses.

6. The price has already been calculated in such a way that we can't provide specialized packing services free of charge.

VI. Reasons and Suggestions for Improving Future Packing

1. **We feel it necessary to stress the importance of** trustworthy packing for your future deliveries to us.

2. **Considering** the long and friendly relations between us, we refrain from lodging a claim this time.

3. Unfortunately, upon arrival, we found that of the 100 cartons of screws, ten cartons were delivered, damaged, and the contents had spilled, leading to some losses.

4. **We agree that** the loss caused is not your fault.

5. In order to avoid any similar incidents, **we feel it necessary to** clarify the concrete stipulations for our future dealings.

6. **We require that** the future packing be in wooden cases of 20 kilos net each, with each wooden case containing 40 cardboard packs of 500 grams net. Each wooden case should be furnished with a handle.

7. **We trust that** you can meet the above requirements and thank you in advance for your cooperation.

VII. Expectations for Further Contact

1. **We trust** this order will be the first of a series of deals between us.

2. **We are looking forward to** your reply for confirmation.

We look forward to your confirmation and shipping advice.

3. Your special attention to the packing will **be greatly appreciated**.

4. **We are awaiting** more orders from you.

5. **Please let us know** whether these specifications can be met by you and whether they will lead to an increase in your prices.

Exercises

I. Choose the best answer to complete each of the following sentences.

1. Thank you for your _____ shipment _____ the goods under our order No. 402 and your S/C No. 702.

 A. quick, for   B. timely, of   C. right, with   D. prompt, in

2. Our packing requirement is that the future _____ be in wooden cases of 50 kilos net each, with each wooden case containing 40 cardboard _____ of 500 grams net.

 A. packing, pack   B. packing, packs

 C. pack, packs   D. packing, packed

3. We agree that each wooden case is _____ with a handle.

 A. packed   B. packing   C. pack   D. package

4. The shirts are packed _____ polybags each as the inner packing and one polybag in a paper box, and 10 dozen boxes in a carton _____ a waterproof sheet.

 A. with, packed with   B. with, wrapped in

 C. into, surrounded with   D. in, lined with

5. We trust that you can meet the above requirements and thank you _____ advance _____ your cooperation.

 A. for, with   B. in, with   C. in, for   D. for, in

6. In order to avoid _____ the importing country's regulations on outer packing material, we would like to make clear our packing requirements as follows.

 A. breaking   B. violating   C. destroying   D. ruining

7. We would like to _____ our order for 800 dozen Rainbow sweaters and your sales confirmation No. SW1708.

 A. refer to   B. referring to   C. refer   D. referring

8. Particular _____ should be _____ the packing of the goods to be delivered in the initial order.

 A. care, taken of   B. attention, paid

 C. care, taken about   D. attention, pay to

9. After _____ the contract, we find that the packing clause in it is not clear enough.

 A. going about   B. going after   C. going into   D. going through

10. We shall be _____ it if you will _____ us of the condition of packing as well as the arrival

of the consignment _____ your end.

  A. glad, tell, at   B. appreciate, talk, in

  C. appreciated, inform, at   D. please, inform, in

II. Fill in the blanks with the appropriate words or expressions.

 1. The metal parts are required to be protected _____ dampness and rust in _____ by a coating of anti-rust grease.

 2. It is the usual _____ here that such goods are packed _____ strong seaworthy wooden cases, _____ with a waterproof sheet.

 3. We believe that the consignment will reach you safe and sound, and the goods will _____ _____ to be satisfactory.

 4. In order to _____ possible future troubles, we would like to _____ clear our packing requirements as _____.

 5. The folding umbrellas _____ the captioned contract should be _____ in paper boxes, each to a box, 40 boxes _____ an export cardboard, and 20 cardboards _____ a wooden case.

III. Give the English/Chinese equivalents of the following expressions.

1. 此面朝上 ＿＿＿＿＿＿＿＿＿   2. 包装说明 ＿＿＿＿＿＿＿＿＿

3. 外包装 ＿＿＿＿＿＿＿＿＿   4. 内包装 ＿＿＿＿＿＿＿＿＿

5. 纸箱 ＿＿＿＿＿＿＿＿＿   6. 板条箱 ＿＿＿＿＿＿＿＿＿

7. 木箱 ＿＿＿＿＿＿＿＿＿   8. 麻布袋 ＿＿＿＿＿＿＿＿＿

9. liquid goods ＿＿＿＿＿＿＿＿   10. carboy ＿＿＿＿＿＿＿＿＿

11. five-ply paper bag ＿＿＿＿＿   12. waterproof foam sheet ＿＿＿＿

13. side marks ＿＿＿＿＿＿＿＿   14. flammable, explosive, poisonous, radioactive goods ＿＿＿＿＿＿＿＿

IV. Translate the following sentences into English/Chinese.

 1. 在外包装上，请标注"小心轻放"字样。

 2. 由于在这里可能会发生对箱子进行野蛮搬运的行为，你方务必确保包装足够结实以保护好货物。

 3. 不同型号的手套绝对不可以混放在同一箱子里。每一个包装中的手套应该是同一型号的。

 4. The touch screens, individually wrapped in waterproof foam sheets, are surrounded by soft padding and packed into small tin boxes, each measuring 16cm×8cm×5cm.

5. Unfortunately, upon arrival, we found that of the 100 cartons of screws, ten cartons were delivered, damaged, and the contents had spilled, leading to some losses.

V. Complete the gaps below with the appropriate words.

Letter 1

Dear Sirs,

　　__1__ reply to your e-mail message of June 18th, we regret to __2__ you that we have forgotten to mention the inner packing __3__ of the Lotus Brand Coffee Bean we ordered __4__ the Guangzhou Spring Fair this year. Now we have discussed the matter with our customers. They require as __5__ :

　　As coffee beans are moisture absorbent especially in hot rainy seasons, it should be __6__ in kraft paper bags __7__ 15 small paper bags of 1 kilogram net each, two kraft paper bags to a carton __8__ with a waterproof paper.

　　We hope the above requirements will be __9__ to you and look forward __10__ your early reply.

　　　　　　　　　　　　　　　　　　　　　　　　Yours sincerely,
　　　　　　　　　　　　　　　　　　　　　　　　×××

Letter 2

Dear Sirs,

　　We regret to inform you that __1__ the 50 cases of auto parts you __2__ to New York on June 16, four were seriously __3__ . Considering the long and friendly __4__ between us, we refrain from lodging a __5__ this time. But we feel it necessary to stress the importance of trustworthy __6__ for your future __7__ to us.

　　As auto parts are susceptible to shock, they must be __8__ in soft materials and firmly __9__ in seaworthy cases in such a manner that the movement inside the cases is impossible. The metal parts should be __10__ from dampness and rust in transit by a coating of anti-rust grease.

　　We trust that you can meet the above requirements and thank you in advance for your cooperation.

　　　　　　　　　　　　　　　　　　　　　　　　Yours sincerely,
　　　　　　　　　　　　　　　　　　　　　　　　×××

Unit 7 Packing

VI. Translate the following letter into Chinese.

Dear Mr. Chen,

We are writing to confirm the packing as follows:

1. Each piece of the goods should be packed in a kraft paper bag, one piece in a waterproof polybag, and 50 pieces packed in one carton.

2. Strong cartons are essential to pack the goods with the size measuring 60cm×45cm×80cm.

3. Ropes or metal handles should be fixed to the cartons to facilitate carrying.

4. Please be sure to put the stuffing materials at the bottom of the cartons.

5. All cartons are stenciled with shipping marks, indicative and warning marks as usual.

We hope that the packing turns out to be satisfactory to our customers. Thank you for your cooperation and look forward to your early reply.

Yours sincerely,

×××

VII. Writing

1. You, Larry, place an order for 1,000 MT red dates with Edwin, requiring shipment to be made not later than September 30th. Since this is the initial order, you are now writing a letter, requesting the red dates to be packed in polybags, each with 250 grams. And 100 bags should be put in a carton. The carton measures 80cm×70cm×50cm each, and it should be lined with plastic sheet and reinforced with two fiber straps.

2. You (Carl Wu) got a letter from your customer, Mike Stephenson, saying that the packing for garments is not good enough. Now you are writing to tell him that you have improved your packing and that from now on all garments are to be packed in cartons instead of wooden cases.

微课视频

扫一扫，获取本课相关微课视频。

7.1.1 Case Study.mp4   7.1.2 Relevant Information.mp4   7.1.3 Writing Skills.mp4

7.2.1　Letter 1 Buyer's Packing Proposal.mp4　　7.2.2　Letter 2 Buyer's Packing Instructions.mp4　　7.2.3　Letter 3 Informing the Details of Packing.mp4

Unit 8   Payment

8.1   Background Knowledge

8.1.1   Case Study

1. Case One

Suppose you are the sales manager of an international export company specializing in skincare and cosmetics products. In your business, what is your preferred payment method? Why? For payment by L/C, what information involving payment will be exchanged between the two parties?

2. Case Two

Suppose you have received the following letter. Why did the seller write to you? What will you write in your reply?

To: "Gloria" <fordbrucecosmeticsinc@gmail.com>
From: "Dolly" <goodwindegqcoltd@hotmail.com>
Subject: Our S/C No. SC202407098 for Skin Care and Body Wash Products
Dear Gloria, With reference to your Order No. ST20240709 and our S/C No. SC202407098, we wish to draw your attention to the fact that the shipment is scheduled for August, 2024 and the covering L/C should reach us not later than July 15th, 2024. We still have not received any information of the L/C from you.

As the goods have been ready for shipment for quite some time and the delivery date is drawing near, please expedite and inform us of the establishment of the L/C so that we can effect shipment within the stipulated time.

We are expecting your L/C and thanks for your cooperation.

Yours faithfully,

Dolly White

Sales Manager

8.1.2 Relevant Information

Terms of payment mean ways or methods of making payment. As they have much to do with the interests and benefits of both the buyer and the seller, they should be agreed upon during the negotiation of a transaction and be explicitly laid down in the contract.

In international trade, buyers and sellers are in two countries. Sometimes, they have to do business with unknown traders. If the seller delivers goods before payment has been made, he/she runs certain risks of non-payment by the buyer; and if the buyer makes payment in advance, he/she likewise runs risks of non-delivery of the goods. Thus, it becomes necessary for a third party to act as an intermediate between them to solve the problem of payment. If so, the bank usually plays this role, either guaranteeing payment to the seller and examining the seller's shipping documents for the buyer, or making collection for the seller, as the seller's principal. So, payment plays a vital role in international trade, which, if not ensured, will result in the total failure of the transaction.

The three most widely accepted terms of payment are payment by L/C, remittance and collection. As to the choice of the payment terms, it all depends. Remittance and collection belong to commercial credit, while L/C belongs to the banker's credit.

1. Payment by L/C

Among the methods to make payment in international trade, the most generally used is Letter of Credit (L/C), which is reliable for both sellers and buyers. It is a written document given by a bank to the exporter at the request of the importer, promising to make payment for a certain amount provided that the seller conforms exactly to the conditions laid down in it. And it is a reliable and safe payment mode facilitating trade with unknown buyers and giving protection to both sellers and buyers. Thus, L/C not only gives protection to both the exporter and the importer but also renders monetary assistance to both of them.

There are different types of L/C, but irrevocable sight (after sight) L/C or irrevocable confirmed sight (after sight) L/C is the most widely accepted. The most newly developed payment procedure is SWIFT, known for its uniform format, fast transfer and low cost.

Letters regarding payment by L/C often fall into the following types: informing the opening of L/C, urging establishment of L/C, amending L/C or asking for extension of L/C, if necessary.

2. Payment by Remittance

In international trade, remittance means that the buyer, on his/her own initiative, remits money to the seller through a correspondent bank. It can be divided into Mail Transfer (M/T), Telegraphic Transfer (T/T) and Demand Draft (D/D) respectively. Remittance service is often used for advance payment, cash on delivery, open account, down payment, payment in installments and commission, etc. In such circumstances, the transactions are rather small and the finance involved is small, too.

3. Payment by Collection

Collection is the presentation of an obligation for payment and the payment thereof. Under collection, the exporter authorizes the bank to collect money from the importer. Upon the delivery of the goods, the exporter draws a bill of exchange on the importer for the sum due. There are two types of collection: Documents against Payment (D/P) and Documents against Acceptance (D/A). According to the different time of payment, D/P can be further divided into D/P at sight and D/P after sight.

In many cases, two or more methods are adopted for one transaction: remittance may be combined with L/C, L/C with collection, etc. Sometimes, under installments or deferred payment for large equipment transactions, a combination of payment methods including L/C, remittance and collection is used. Down payment, advance payment, cash on delivery, cash with order, etc. are also used accordingly.

8.1.3 Writing Skills

1. Writing Skills of Letters Proposing Payment Method

Terms of payment have much to do with the interests and benefits of both the buyer and the seller. The two parties hope to get their favorable terms, so they would give proposal of payment, trying to persuade the other party into accepting it. In such a letter, the following skills are usually suggested:

(1) Courtesy: Take the "You Attitude", not "We Attitude", expressing thanks for the cooperation at the very beginning, then expressing your strong expectation with your heartfelt sincerity to conclude the mutually beneficial deal.

(2) Directness: Make your proposal and give your reasons directly and clearly and avoid giving too much other information to distract the recipient's attention. Just focus on the subject, but leave room for negotiation.

(3) Persuasiveness: Use the persuading tone to talk the recipient into accepting your terms of payment, emphasizing and encouraging the other party that it is a mutually beneficial transaction.

2. Writing Skills of Letters in Reply to Payment Proposal

When receiving a letter of payment proposal, whether to accept or not, the recipient should consider the following skills:

(1) Promptness: Respond immediately with your "Yes" or "No" answer to the proposal and express your thanks for the proposal.

(2) Consideration: For a "Yes" reply, express your pleasure in the cooperation. And for a "No" answer, show your regret, give a new proposal, and provide the reasons.

(3) Courtesy and encouragement: Use courteous and encouraging words in your reply to facilitate mutual acceptance so as to help your refusal to be understood and your new proposal to be accepted.

3. Writing Skills of Letters Urging Establishment of L/C

If the buyer and the seller agree on L/C payment terms, after the acknowledgement of the order and the signing of the contract, the buyer, as a rule, is under obligation to open a letter of credit with his/her bank within the contractual time. However, there may be circumstances where the buyer fails to establish L/C, or it does not reach the seller in time. Then, a letter, or a fax has to be sent to the buyer to urge him/her to expedite the L/C or to ascertain its whereabouts. In such correspondence, the writer should take such skills as:

(1) **Courtesy:** Take "You attitude" to pen the letter in a positive way and with a polite tone, showing your gratitude, directly referring to the problem that the goods ordered are ready but the relevant letter of credit has not yet been received without anything reserved.

(2) **Conventionality:** To urge an establishment of L/C, you should comply with the agreement, remind the buyer to open the L/C as required and make sure the L/C is in exact accordance with the S/C.

(3) **Seriousness:** State clearly the consequences resulted in for delay opening/receiving of L/C with a slightly strong but quite definite tone. If the first message brings no reply, send a second one immediately to express your disappointment and surprise.

4. Writing Skills of L/C Amendment/Extension Letters

When examining the L/C, if there is any discrepancy, the exporter should immediately contact the importer and request the latter to arrange with the issuing bank to send an amendment as required. Sometimes an unexpected situation regarding supply, shipping, etc. may arise. In this case, the seller asks for extension of the expiry date of the L/C as well as the date of shipment and an amendment to the original L/C will be required.

In writing such a letter, the following skills are advisable:

(1) **Conciseness:** Get to the point, describing the problem in detail and giving your requirements directly, clearly and definitely. It is advisable to make a list of your requirements for amendment one by one.

(2) **Courtesy and friendliness:** Actively find the way to solve the problem with a courteous and friendly tone for such a costly and annoying matter. Regardless of whose carelessness or fault causes the trouble, don't complain, because complaining does no good in solving the problems.

(3) **Encouragement:** Emphasize that your incentive or encouragement to the buyer for a quick amendment is for the sake of a mutually beneficial transaction and express your expectation for more future business.

Not only can the seller ask for amendment to an L/C, the buyer can likewise ask for amendment if he finds anything in the L/C needs to be altered. The usual procedure is that the buyer should first obtain consent from the seller and then instruct the opening bank to amend the L/C. The principles above can be applicable, too.

8.2 Sample Letters and Basic Writing Structure Analysis

8.2.1 Basic Writing Structures of Letters Concerning Terms of Payment Proposal

In a letter concerning terms of payment, the following structure is often used:

1. Express thanks and mention the important information;

2. Put forward the terms of payment, and give the reason(s) for your suggestion or your refusal of other payment methods;

3. Emphasize the importance of payment arrangement;

4. Close the letter by expressing expectations of an early reply or suggesting future business dealings.

Letter 1 Seller's Proposal for Payment

To: "Cheney"<forestcosmeticsinc@gmail.com>
From: "Dennis" <charminghcoltd@hotmail.com>
Subject: Terms of Payment

Dear Cheney,

Thank you for the Purchase Confirmation No. BC123 of August 8th, ordering our bath products and cosmetic products. We are definitely able to meet your delivery date.

Our usual mode of payment is by confirmed, irrevocable letter of credit, available by draft at sight for the full amount of the invoice value to be established through a bank acceptable to us.

On receipt of your covering L/C, we will make arrangements for shipment of your order. For any information or questions, please do not hesitate to contact us.

Your kindness in giving priority to the consideration of the above requests and giving us an early favorable reply would be highly appreciated.

With best regards,

Yours sincerely,

Dennis Weber

Overseas Sales Director

In a reply to the other party's payment proposal, the recipient should make clear his/her attitude whether to accept the proposal or to give a new proposal. Such a letter usually contains the following contents:

1. Expressing thanks for the letter;

2. Refusing the terms proposed, offer new terms and state the reasons;

3. Expecting the acceptance of the new terms.

Letter 2   A Reply to Seller's Payment Proposal

To: "Dennis" <charminghcoltd@hotmail.com>
From: "Cheney"<forestcosmeticsinc@gmail.com>
Subject: Terms of Payment

Dear Dennis,

Thank you for your letter of August 2nd, 2023 on payment arrangement of the Sales Confirmation No. BC123.

We would like to pay for this order by a 30-day L/C. This is our customary practice. This order involves US$80,000 and since we have only moderate cash reserves, tying up funds for 1 or 2 months would be inconvenient for us. In this case, we regret that we cannot meet your wishes.

We would very much appreciate your cooperation and would be most grateful if you could accept our proposal. If you are agreeable, please send us your contract. On receipt, we will establish the relevant L/C.

Yours sincerely,

Cheney Lane

Overseas Purchasing Director

8.2.2 Basic Writing Structures of Letters Urging Establishment of L/C

As trade practice, only when the seller receives the right L/C, can he/she make shipment of the goods ordered. If the L/C fails to reach the seller at the due time, the seller will urge the buyer to expedite the opening of the L/C. The letter will contain the following contents:

1. Refer to the transaction, informing the buyer that the goods ordered are ready or the shipping space has been booked but the relevant L/C has not come to hand;

2. Then, politely push the buyer to open the L/C by referring to the stipulations of the contract or by reminding the buyer of the seriousness of not opening the L/C in time;

3. Finally, express expectations and ask the buyer to take immediate actions.

Letter 3   Urging the Establishment of L/C

To: "Cheney"<forestcosmeticsinc@gmail.com>
From: "Dennis" <charminghcoltd@hotmail.com>
Subject: Sales Confirmation No. BC123

Dear Cheney,

With reference to the Sales Confirmation No. BC123 of August 6th for our bath products and cosmetics products, we wish to draw your attention to the fact that the date of delivery is approaching, but we still have not received your covering Letter of Credit to date.

We wish to remind you that it was agreed, when you placed the order, that you would establish the required L/C upon receipt of our confirmation.

Please do your utmost to expedite the opening of the L/C, so that we may execute the order smoothly. In order to avoid subsequent amendments, please see to it that the L/C stipulations are in exact accordance with the terms of the contract.

We hope to receive your favorable news soon.

With best regards,

Yours sincerely,

Dennis Weber

Overseas Sales Director

8.2.3　Basic Writing Structures of Letters Notifying the Establishment of L/C

After opening the L/C through the issuing bank, the buyer should spare no time to inform the seller of it. Such a letter often includes the following steps:

1. Mention the former letter concerning the opening of L/C;

2. Advise the seller that you have opened the relevant L/C (mention the name of the issuing bank, L/C number, its amount and validity);

3. Stress the documents required for negotiation: state clear what shipping documents are to be accompanied with the draft when the seller makes their negotiation at the bank;

4. Express your expectations that the ordered goods will arrive at your place in due time.

Letter 4　Notifying the Establishment of L/C

To: "Dennis" <charminghcoltd@hotmail.com>
From: "Cheney"<forestcosmeticsinc@gmail.com>
Subject: Sales Confirmation No. BC123

Dear Dennis,

We have pleasure in receiving your letter of August 8th concerning the opening of the covering L/C.

We are glad to inform you that a confirmed, irrevocable L/C No. 1708101 has been established in your favor through the Commercial Bank of San Francisco on August 10th, 2023 for USD 80,000. The credit will be confirmed by the Bank of China, Guangzhou Branch.

The credit will remain valid until September 10th, 2023. The documents required for the negotiation are as follows:

  three copies of Commercial Invoices

  two copies of Bill of Lading

  one original Insurance Policy

Please make arrangements to effect shipment before September 10th, 2023 and advise us by e-mail when the goods have been shipped.

Yours sincerely,

Cheney Lane

Overseas Purchasing Director

8.2.4 Basic Writing Structures of L/C Amendment Letters

  If the exporter finds some discrepancies in the L/C or if he/she fails to get the goods ready for the shipment in time or the importer requests that shipment be postponed for some reason, he/she will have to ask for amendment of the L/C. The following structure is useful for his/her reference in writing such a letter:

  1. Acknowledge the receipt of the L/C and thank the buyer for opening it;

  2. State the problem and give the reasons for amendment;

  3. End the letter in a way to encourage the buyer to take immediate action;

  4. Urge a prompt reply.

Letter 5 L/C Amendment

To: "Cheney"<forestcosmeticsinc@gmail.com>
From: "Dennis" <charminghcoltd@hotmail.com>
Subject: L/C No. 1708101 for Bath Products and Cosmetic Products

Dear Cheney,

We received your above L/C with thanks, but we regret to inform you that we found some discrepancies against the S/C. Please make amendment as follows:

1. The price term should be CIF San Diego, USA.
2. Transshipment is to be allowed.
3. Extend the latest shipping date to August 26th, 2023 and the validity to September 25th, 2023.

We shall be glad if you will see to it that amendment is faxed without delay, as our goods have been packed ready for shipment for quite some time.

To show our sincerity, we will pay for the amendment charge. We are really sorry for the trouble caused and appreciate your great help on the matter.

We are looking forward to your amendment soon.

With best regards,

Yours sincerely,

Dennis Weber

Overseas Sales Director

Useful Words & Expressions

I. Widely-used Terms

1. date of shipment 装运日期	2. covering L/C	相关的信用证
3. delivery date 交货日期	4. establishment of the L/C	开立信用证
5. effect shipment 发货	6. mode of payment	付款方式
7. full amount 全额	8. L/C stipulations	信用证的规定
9. Insurance policy 保险单	10. required L/C	开立所需的信用证
11. invoice value 发票金额	12. 30-day L/C	30 天期信用证
13. Bill of Lading 海运提单	14. commercial invoice	商业发票
15. in one's favor / in the favor of	以……为受益人	

II. Important Phrases

1. with reference to   关于
2. draw one's attention to   提醒某人注意
3. draw near   临近
4. stipulated time   规定的时间
5. meet your delivery date   满足你方交货期
6. on receipt of   一收到就
7. make arrangement for shipment   安排装运
8. early favorable reply   早日惠复
9. payment arrangement   付款安排
10. customary practice   惯例
11. moderate cash reserves   适度的现金储备
12. tying up funds   占用资金
13. subsequent amendments   后续的修改
14. accordance with   与……一致
15. see to it   务必要
16. amendment charge   修改费

III. Expressing Thanks and Mentioning Important Information

1. **Thank you for** the Purchase Confirmation No. BC123 of August 8th, ordering our bath products and cosmetic products.

We are definitely able to meet your delivery date.

2. **Thank you for** your letter of August 2nd, 2023 on payment arrangement of the Sales Confirmation No. BC123.

3. **We have pleasure in** receiving your letter of August 8th concerning the opening of the covering L/C.

4. **We received** your above L/C **with thanks**.

IV. Seller's Payment Proposal

1. **Our usual mode of payment is** by confirmed, irrevocable letter of credit, available by draft at sight for the full amount of the invoice value to be established through a bank acceptable to us.

2. On receipt of your covering L/C, we will **make arrangements for shipment** of your order.

3. We adopt (accept) **payment by L/C**.

We refer you to Contract No. 824 prescribing payment by sight L/C.

4. We regret that we are unable to consider your request for **payment under D/A terms**.

5. We are prepared to accept payment for your trial order on D/P basis.

6. **D/P is applicable only if** the amount involved for each transaction is less than USD1,000.

7. Please see to it that payment is made by confirmed, irrevocable L/C **in our favor**, available by draft at sight, and allowing transshipment and partial shipment.

8. Please note that payment is to be made by confirmed, irrevocable L/C allowing **partial shipments** and **transshipment**, available by draft at sight.

9. According to the stipulations in our S/C No. 210, you should send us your L/C one month **preceding the date of shipment**.

10. **Your proposal for** payment by time draft for Order No. 1156 **is acceptable to us**, and we shall draw on you at 60 days' sight after the goods have been shipped. Please honor our draft when it falls due.

11. **Your request** for payment by D/P **has been taken into consideration**. In view of the small amount of this transaction, we are prepared to effect shipment on this basis.

V. Reply to Seller's Payment Proposal

1. **We would like to pay for** this order **by** a 30-day **L/C**. This is our customary practice.

2. This order involves US$80,000 and since we have only moderate cash reserves, tying up funds for 1 or 2 months **would be inconvenient for us**.

3. In this case, **we regret that we cannot** meet your wishes.

4. **We would very much appreciate your cooperation** and would be most grateful if you could accept our proposal.

5. **If you are agreeable, please send us your contract**. On receipt, we will establish the relevant L/C.

6. **It has been our usual practice to do business with payment by D/P at sight instead of by L/C**. We should, therefore, like you to accept D/P terms for this transaction and future ones.

7. **Our usual mode of payment is by confirmed, irrevocable L/C**, available by draft at sight for the full amount of the invoice value to be established in our favor through a bank acceptable to us.

VI. Establishment of L/C

Urging Establishment of L/C (Seller)

1. As the goods have been ready for shipment for quite some time and the delivery date is

drawing near, **please expedite and inform us of the establishment of the L/C,** so that we can effect shipment within the stipulated time.

2. **With reference to** the Sales Confirmation No. BC123 of August 6th for our bath products and cosmetic products, **we wish to draw your attention to the fact that** the date of delivery is approaching, but we still have not received your covering Letter of Credit to date.

3. **We wish to remind you that** it was agreed, when you placed the order, that you would establish the required L/C upon receipt of our confirmation.

4. **Please do your utmost to** expedite the opening of the L/C, so that we may execute the order smoothly. In order to avoid subsequent amendments, please see to it that the L/C stipulations are in exact accordance with the terms of the Contract.

5. Please **expedite the L/C** so that we may execute the order smoothly.

6. The shipment date is approaching. It would be advisable for you to **open the L/C** covering your order No. 751 as early as possible so as to enable us to effect shipment within the stipulated time limit.

Notifying the Establishment of L/C (Buyer)

1. **We are glad to inform you that** a confirmed, irrevocable L/C No. 1708101 has been established in your favor through the Commercial Bank of San Francisco on August 10th, 2023 for USD 80,000.

2. **The credit will be confirmed by** the Bank of China, Guangzhou Branch.

3. **The credit will remain valid until** September 10th, 2023. The documents required for the negotiation are as follows: three copies of Commercial Invoices; two copies of Bill of Lading; one original Insurance Policy.

4. Please make arrangements to effect shipment before September 10th, 2023 and advise us by cable when the goods have been shipped.

5. We have instructed the Bank of Toronto to open a L/C for US$20,000 order No. 25, covering 1000 casks of iron nails in your favor.

We have instructed our bankers, the Standard Chartered Bank, Hong Kong to telegraph the sum of HK$20,000 for the credit of your account at the BOC, Shanghai.

6. In order to cover this order, we have established an irrevocable and confirmed L/C in your favor through Barclays Bank, London for Stg. 45,000.

7. We have opened an irrevocable L/C No. GB418 through the City Bank, NY.

Asking for Amendment of the L/C

1. **We regret to inform you that** we found some discrepancies against the S/C.

2. **Please make amendment as follows:**

(1) The price term should be CIF San Diego, USA.

(2) Transshipment is to be allowed.

(3) Extend the latest shipping date to August 26th, 2023 and the validity to September 25th, 2023.

3. To show our sincerity, we will pay for the amendment charge.

4. **We are really sorry for** the trouble caused and appreciate your great help on the matter.

5. We have extended the shipment and validity dates of the L/C to October 15th and 31st respectively.

The buyer shall pay the total value to the seller in advance by T/T not later than May 15th.

6. **On the examination of the**… we found the following discrepancies/mistakes/points do not conform to the terms contracted.

Therefore please instruct your bank to make the necessary amendments.

VII. Expectations for Further Contact

1. **We are expecting** your L/C and thanks for your cooperation.

2. **Your kindness in** giving priority to the consideration of the above requests **and giving us an early** favorable **reply would be highly appreciated**.

3. **We shall be glad if you** will see to it that amendment is faxed without delay, as our goods have been packed ready for shipment for quite some time.

4. In order to pave the way for your pushing the sale of our products in your market, we will accept payment by D/P at sight as **a special accommodation**.

5. **We hope to** receive your favorable news soon.

6. **We are looking forward to** your amendment soon.

Exercises

I. Choose the best answer to complete each of the following sentences.

1. As requested, we have immediately arranged _____ our bankers to extend the expiry date of our L/C for half a month (up to) 31 July.

    A. with   B. to   C. in   D. for

2. We enclose our cheque for US$500 _____ your invoice No. 1806.

    A. by payment of   B. in payment of

C. to payment on D. for payment in

3. We regret to ask you to open an irrevocable credit _____ and shall hand over shipping documents _____ acceptance of our draft.

A. for our favor, against B. in our favor, by

C. in our favor, against D. in our favor, through

4. We have _____ at 30 days' sight for the amount of the invoice.

A. written to you B. sent to you by e-mail

C. drawn on you D. called on you

5. As the delivery date is _____ near, please expedite and inform us of the establishment of the L/C.

A. going to draw B. drawing C. to draw D. drawn

6. The two companies hope to get their own favorable terms, so they would try to persuade the other party _____ it.

A. accepting B. accept to C. accepting of D. into accepting

7. We still have not received your covering Letter of Credit to date, so we hope you would _____ the agreement.

A. comply B. be complied

C. be complying D. comply with

8. As arranged, we hope to receive your _____ news soon so as to avoid any delay in effecting shipment.

A. reasonable B. favorable C. comfortable D. sensible

9. We are prepared to accept payment _____ confirmed, irrevocable L/C available _____ draft _____ sight instead of T/T reimbursement.

A. by, by, at B. by, by, in C. with, at, at D. with, in, at

10. _____ this matter, we have already written to you.

A. As regard B. With regard to C. In regarding D. Regarding to

II. Fill in the blanks with the appropriate words or expressions.

1. Our usual mode of payment is _____ confirmed, irrevocable letter of credit, available _____ draft _____ sight for the full amount of the invoice value to be established _____ a bank acceptable to us.

2. On _____ of your covering L/C, we will make arrangement _____ shipment of your order. For any information or questions, please do not hesitate to _____ us.

3. Your kindness in giving _____ to the consideration of the above request and giving us an early favorable _____ would be highly _____.

4. We would very much appreciate your _____ and would be most _____ if you could _____ our proposal.

5. _____ reference to the Sales Confirmation No. BC123 of August 6th for our bath products and cosmetic products, we wish to _____ your attention to the fact that the date of delivery is _____.

III. Give the English/Chinese equivalents of the following expressions.

1. 汇票 _____
2. 支票 _____
3. 即期支付 _____
4. 开证行 _____
5. 汇款 _____
6. 托收 _____
7. 定金 _____
8. 分期付款 _____
9. confirmed, irrevocable L/C _____
10. in one's favor _____
11. the extension of L/C _____
12. Documents against Payment (D/P) _____
13. Documents against Acceptance (D/A) _____
14. Telegraphic Transfer (T/T) _____

IV. Translate the following sentences into Chinese/English.

1. Further to your letter of January 18th regarding our Latex Gloves, we would like to accept payment on D/P basis.

2. Our usual terms of payment are by confirmed, irrevocable letter of credit available by draft at sight, accompanied by shipping documents which are to be presented to the negotiating bank at the port of loading.

3. 按照安排，我们已凭单据向你方开具汇票，通过中国银行向你方索取发票金额。

4. 鉴于此笔交易金额较小，我们准备接受即期付款交单(或30天付款交单)向你方收取货款。

V. Complete the gaps with the appropriate words.

Letter 1

Dear Sirs,

We thank you for your letter dated April 25th in which you __1__ to pay by D/A for a trial delivery of our gift boxes.

　　We appreciate your interest in __2__ the sale of our products in your market, but we feel much __3__ that we are unable to consider your __4__ for payment __5__ D/A terms, because in our usual __6__ we generally adopt the method of payment by letter of credit for our exports.

　　Considering our friendly and long business relations, we shall consider accepting the payment, as an exceptional case, 40% deposit, the __7__ before shipment. We hope this __8__ will be conducive to you in procuring more orders for us to our mutual __9__.

　　We look forward to your __10__ reply at an early date.

Yours truly,
× × ×

Letter 2

Dear Danny,

　　We have pleasure in __1__ your letter of February 8th concerning the opening of the covering L/C.

　　We are glad to __2__ you that a confirmed, __3__ L/C No. 280976 has been __4__ in your __5__ through the Commercial Bank of New York on August 28th, 2023 __6__ USD 56,000. The credit will be __7__ by the Bank of China, Hong Kong Branch.

　　The credit will remain __8__ until September 28th, 2023. The documents required for the negotiation are as __9__:

　　three copies of Commercial Invoices

　　two copies of Bill of Lading

　　one original Insurance Policy

　　Please make arrangements to __10__ shipment before September 28th, 2023 and advise us by e-mail when the goods have been shipped.

Yours sincerely,
Linda
Overseas Marketing Director

VI. Translate the following letter into Chinese.

Dear Sirs,

With reference to 2,000 dozen cotton beach shorts under our S/C No. 501, the past purchase from you has been paid as a rule by confirmed, irrevocable letter of credit.

On this basis, we have to point out that it has indeed cost us a great deal. From the moment we open an L/C till the time our buyers pay us, our funds will be returned slowly. Under the present circumstances, we propose payment by Cash against Documents on arrival of goods. If you could kindly make favorable payment terms, we are sure that such an accommodation would be conducive to our business.

We will be grateful for your careful consideration. We await your early reply.

Yours faithfully,

×××

VII. Writing.

Write the following letters according to the situations given below.

1. You, Jessica, place an order for 1,000 pairs of jeans at the price listed in the catalogue No. J123, USD 40 per pair, requiring the goods to be shipped not later than October 20th. You would like to pay for the order by a sixty-day L/C. And you give your reasons for such a payment proposal. Now, please write the letter to your seller, Martin, expecting he can accept your proposal.

2. You, Judy, received the L/C No. V-162 opened by the Chartered Bank of Liverpool under our S/C No. 968, but when examining the L/C, you found some discrepancies:

(1) 3% commission, not 5%;

(2) shipment during November/December, not "on or before November 30th";

(3) insurance value of 110% of the invoice value, not 150%;

Now, you write to the importer, Robert, requesting him to make amendments.

微课视频

扫一扫,获取本课相关微课视频。

8.1.1　Case Study.mp4

8.1.2　Relevant Information.mp4

8.1.3　Writing Skills.mp4

8.2.1　Letter 1 Seller's Proposal for Payment.mp4

8.2.1　Letter 2 A Reply to Seller's Payment Proposal.mp4

8.2.2　Letter 3 Urging the Establishment of L/C.mp4

8.2.3　Letter 4 Notifying the Establishment of L/C.mp4

8.2.4　Letter 5 L/C Amendment.mp4

Unit 9   Shipment

9.1   Background Knowledge

9.1.1   Case Study

1. Case One

Suppose you are a businessperson in the field of accessories export. Now, you are undergoing the procedure of shipment in correspondence exchange. Generally speaking, what information concerning shipment of the goods will be exchanged between you and the buyer?

2. Case Two

Suppose your colleague Marcy receives the following letter. Why does the buyer send her this letter? How will she write the reply letter?

To: "Marcy" <woodjcarloinc@gmail.com>   **From:** "Elvis" <brooks company@hotmail.com>   **Subject:** 3,000 Pieces of White Metal Hair Accessories Under S/C No. WH17073
Dear Marcy,   Referring to the subject goods, we very much regret that up to now, we have not heard anything about shipment from you about this lot.   As the selling season is rapidly approaching, our buyers here are urging us for early delivery. We shall be very much grateful if you can effect shipment as soon as possible, thus enabling them to

catch the brisk demand.

We would like to emphasize that any delay in shipping our order will undoubtedly involve us in no small difficulty.

We await your immediate reply.

Yours faithfully,

Elvis

Purchasing Manager

9.1.2 Relevant Information

Shipment, as one of the important terms of a sales contract, means that the seller fulfills his/her obligation by delivering the goods to the buyer or loading the goods on the named carrier at the specified place and the time stipulated in the contract. In international trade, goods can be delivered by road, rail, air or sea. In spite of different modes of transportation, ocean transportation is the most widely used form for its low cost and large capacity.

1. The Shipment Clause

The shipment clause is an integral and important part of a sales contract. It includes the time of shipment, the ports of loading and destination, modes of transportation and the shipping documents, partial shipment, transshipment, etc., which should be explicitly stipulated in the sales contract.

2. Shipping Instructions

When placing the order, or more often after the order is confirmed, buyers generally send their shipping instructions to the sellers, informing them in writing of the mode of transportation, core information of the order, the packing, shipping date, shipping marks, etc., which is known as the Shipping Instructions. Meanwhile, the sellers usually send a Shipping Advice to the buyers as soon as the goods are loaded on board the ship, advising them of the shipment.

3. Shipping Advice

Shipping Advice, also known as shipping statement, or shipment details, is a note usually sent by the exporter to the importer when the goods are loaded on board the vessel, informing of the particulars of shipment, helping the importer to take out insurance or to facilitate the arrangement of storage, payment and taking delivery of the goods accordingly, etc.

It gives a detailed description of the shipment including the name of the shipping vessel, the shipping date or the ETD/ETA, the departure port and destination, the packing, name and quantity of the goods, the B/L number, the invoice number and amount, the order number, the S/C number and/or L/C number, etc.

Nowadays, Shipping Advice is often sent by fax or e-mail. If there is a stipulation regarding this in the L/C and/or the Contract, the seller should by no means neglect it. He/she must fulfill his/her obligations by giving the shipping advice in strict accordance with the stipulation, which is used as a negotiating document to be delivered to the bank.

4. Shipping Documents

When shipment is effected, the seller must deliver to the buyer a complete set of shipping documents as a sign of his/her performance of the contract and the basis of his/her negotiaton. As to the types of the documents and the number of each of them, they are to be agreed upon by the buyer and the seller in a specific transaction.

When goods are transported by road, rail, or air, the contract of the carriage takes the form of a consignment note or railway bill of lading or air waybill. In sea transport, an ocean bill of lading or a charter party is adopted instead.

9.1.3 Writing Skills

1. Writing Skills of Letters about Shipping Instructions

In international trade, when it comes to shipment, the two parties have come to terms on most aspects of the transaction. A successful business is almost secured. So, correspondence exchange concerning shipment usually takes a pleasant and delightful tune. The following skills can always be found in good letters about shipping instructions.

(1) Courtesy: Start the letter in a pleasant way, expressing thanks for the cooperation. For a transaction with payment by L/C, bring good news about the opening of the L/C.

(2) Completeness and Conciseness: Give your shipping instructions in great detail, making sure not to miss anything important. Meanwhile, you should remember to give your instructions explicitly and directly and avoid anything unrelated, strictly observing the stipulations in the contract and concentrating on the topic of shipping instruction.

(3) Encouragement: End the letter by expressing good wishes to encourage the other party to cooperate and take immediate actions, sincerely expecting shipment to be made smoothly and more future business to be done.

2. Writing Skills of Letters about Urging an Early Shipment

Shipment should be made as contracted. If not, the buyer will contact the seller, urging an early shipment. But sometimes, the buyer, required by his/her clients, may ask for an early shipment on his/her own. Or the seller cannot deliver the goods in time due to various reasons. Here are the usual skills for such writings:

(1) Courtesy and consideration: Express your thanks for the business and urge an early shipment. Ask the reason for the delay in shipment with a friendly tone and promise to offer help if needed.

(2) Relevance: Refer the recipient to your previous correspondence or your contract or order as a reminder and say that you haven't got any news about the shipment of the goods.

(3) Highlight: Emphasize the importance of timely shipment and express your thanks for cooperation. If you ask for an early shipment for your own benefit, give your acceptable reasons and try to talk your recipient into accepting your requirement with a persuasive and polite tone.

3. Writing Skills of Letters about Giving Shipping Advice

Shipping advice plays a vital role in helping the importer to take out insurance or to facilitate the arrangement of storage, payment and taking delivery of the goods, etc. In writing a letter about shipping advice, such skills should be followed:

(1) Pleasure: Take a pleasing tone to advise the buyer that the goods have been shipped and express your thanks for the order and cooperation.

(2) Completeness: Provide all the shipping details, including the name of the vessel, the port of shipment, the core information of the order, the contract number, the packing, ETD and ETA, etc. The detailed documents to be dispatched should also be listed. Any omission or error may lead to inconvenience or even failure in delivery.

(3) Sincerity: Express your hope for a satisfactory shipment to the buyer, assure him/her of your assistance whenever he/she needs and expects more future business.

9.2 Sample Letters and Basic Writing Structure Analysis

9.2.1 Basic Writing Structures of Letters Concerning Sending Shipping Instructions

Before shipment, the buyers generally send shipping instructions to the sellers, informing them of shipping requirements, packing requirements and marks, etc.

1. Tell the recipient (seller) that the relevant L/C has been opened.
2. Give some instructions concerning the date of shipment, name of the vessel, or the quality of the goods, etc.
3. Express your good wishes or show your expectations for the shipping advice.

Letter 1 Sending Shipping Instructions

To: "Denny" <greatjewelrycaicoltd@hotmail.com>
From: "Jeff" <fordkvtradeinc@gmail.com>
Subject: Order No. P/O170802 for 5,000 Pieces Imitation Jewelry

Dear Denny,

With reference to the captioned goods, we are glad to inform you that the relevant L/C was opened yesterday and it is on the way to you.

We have booked shipping space on S.S. "Great Victory" which is scheduled to sail from Sete, France to Xingang, Tianjin around the end of next month. Please get the goods ready for shipment early. Jewelry is fragile, and special care should be taken during shipment.

On the attached list are particulars of packing and shipping marks, which must be strictly observed.

Your early shipping advice will be highly appreciated.

With best regards,

Yours sincerely,

Jeff Pond

Overseas Purchasing Director

9.2.2 Basic Writing Structures of Letters Concerning Urging an Early Shipment

An early shipment is usually mutually beneficial, but for one reason or another, sometimes, shipment can't be effected as expected. In such circumstances, the buyer will write to the seller, urging an early shipment. Here are the usual structures for such letters:

1. Indicate the relevant order and its order number as a reminder and raise the problem directly;

2. Ask the recipient to send the goods punctually and give the reasons;

3. State your hope for punctual shipment.

Letter 2　Urging an Early Shipment

To: "Denny"<greatjewelrycaicoltd@hotmail.com>
From: "Jeff"<fordkvtradeinc@gmail.com>
Subject: Order No. P/O170802 for 5,000 Pieces Imitation Jewelry

Dear Denny,

We are now eager to know about the shipment of our order No. P/O170802 for 5,000 pieces of imitation jewelry. The shipment date is approaching, but we still have not had any news about it since the L/C No. 1708 was issued two weeks ago.

With this letter, we wish to draw your attention to the fact that the L/C will expire at the end of next week and that we are not going to extend it. And our clients are in urgent need of the goods, so we cannot afford to wait any longer. Therefore, we will have to resort to other sources of imitation jewelry suppliers if you fail to make the shipment in due time.

We believe that all parties involved would definitely benefit from your prompt action of the shipment. We are looking forward to receiving your shipping advice.

Yours sincerely, Jeff Pond Overseas Purchasing Manager

9.2.3 Basic Writing Structures of Reply Letters to Urging an Early Shipment

After receiving the letter urging shipment, the seller will spare no time to make a reply. If it is a favorable reply, it is likely to be a shipping advice, or else, emphasis should be laid on the reasons for the delay in shipment and a promise to take immediate actions.

Therefore, the favorable reply to an urging shipment often includes the following parts:

1. Inform the importer of the shipment;
2. State details of shipment;
3. Give positive responses and express anticipation for future orders.

Letter 3　A Favorable Reply to the Letter above

To: "Jeff"<fordkvtradeinc@gmail.com> **From:** "Denny"<greatjewelrycaicoltd@hotmail.com> **Subject:** Order No. P/O170802 for 5,000 Pieces Imitation Jewelry
Dear Jeff, With reference to your letter of August 6th, 2023, urging our prompt action of shipment, we are now glad to inform you that the 5,000 pieces of imitation jewelry have been shipped. The consignment has been on board S.S. "Great Victory", which will set out sailing for your port tomorrow morning. To offer more detailed information about the shipment, tomorrow morning we will fax you the copy of B/L, the original of which is, together with other documents required by the L/C, being passed to you through the negotiating bank and the issuing bank. We are pleased that we have been able to execute your order within the contracted valid period this time, and would like to express our strong willingness to pay even more prompt attention to your future orders.

With best regards,

Yours sincerely,

Denny Wang

Overseas Sales Director

However, the unfavorable reply to urging shipment usually means delay shipment. In such a case, the seller should take the initiative to explain the reasons for the delay and the current progress of shipment arrangement. So, such letters often include the following parts:

1. Express appreciation for the previous letter;
2. Apologize for the delay in shipment and state the reasons;
3. State the scheduled time for shipment;
4. Apologize again and express hope for future cooperation.

Letter 4   Delay Shipment

To: "Jeff"<fordkvtradeinc@gmail.com>
From: "Denny"<greatjewelrycaicoltd@hotmail.com>
Subject: Order No. P/O170802 for 5,000 Pieces Imitation Jewelry

Dear Jeff,

Thank you for your letter dated August 6th, 2023, asking for definite news of shipment of the subject goods.

We must apologize for the delay delivery of your order, which has been caused by the unexpected late arrival of goods from the place of origin.

Now the shipment has been arranged to go forth on board S.S. "Pigeon", which is scheduled to sail for you early next week. We are sorry for not contacting you timely. We promise to advise you details of the shipment once the goods are placed on board the steamer.

It is sincerely hoped that our delay in communicating with you on the above order has caused you no trouble and that shipment will turn out to be completely satisfactory. We would apologize again for the inconvenience caused and if there is any loss sustained due to our delay, we will compensate you.

We assure you that any order from you in the future will get our prompt attention. We are awaiting your future cooperation.

Yours sincerely,

Denny Wang

Overseas Sales Director

9.2.4 Basic Writing Structures of Letters Concerning Shipping Advice

The basic function of a shipping advice is to inform the buyer of the detailed shipment information and the relevant documents dispatched. Therefore, such letters usually contain the following parts:

1. Express thanks for the order and mention the shipment;
2. Give detailed information about the shipment, such as the shipping date, the name of vessel, core information of the order, the contract number, the packing, the shipping company, ETD and ETA, and so on;
3. List the detailed shipping documents covering the deal;
4. Express hope for more business in the future.

Letter 5　Shipping Advice

To: "Jeff"<fordkvtradeinc@gmail.com>
From: "Denny"<greatjewelrycaicoltd@hotmail.com>
Subject: Shipment of Order No. P/O170802 under L/C No. 1708

Dear Jeff,

Thank you for your order for the 5,000 pieces of imitation Jewelry. We have pleasure in informing you that, in accordance with the stipulations set forth in the captioned letter of credit, today we have shipped the goods on board S.S. "Great Victory" which will sail for your port tomorrow.

We have airmailed one set of the shipping documents covering this deal as follows:
Our Invoice No. T-F38695 in duplicate
Packing List No. 89623 in duplicate
Non-negotiable Bill of Lading No. IJ8769
Insurance Policy No. TJ0363879
Certificate of Quality No. TJIJ3865
The original documents will be sent to you through our bank.

We trust the above shipment will reach you in safe and sound condition and expect to receive your further orders. We take this opportunity to appreciate the business between us and assure you of our best attention to your future orders.

Yours sincerely,

Denny

Overseas Sales Director

Sometimes, if the goods ordered can't be shipped as a whole lot, partial shipment has to be chosen; then there will be partial shipment shipping advice as shown in the following letter.

Letter 6   Partial Shipment Shipping Advice

To: "Denny"<fordkvtradeinc@gmail.com>
From: "Jeff" <greatjewelrycaicoltd@hotmail.com>
Subject: Your Order No. P/O170802 for 5,000 Pieces Imitation Jewelry

Dear Denny,

Thank you for your order for the 5,000 pieces of imitation Jewelry. We have pleasure in informing you that, in accordance with our supplementary agreement, we have shipped in partial fulfillment of the captioned order, 1,000 necklaces, pendants and earrings respectively, per S.S. "Great Victory" which will sail for your port tomorrow.

We have airmailed all the copy documents. The original documents will be sent to you through our bank.

As for the remaining 1,000 gold plating bracelets and 1,000 anklets, we will endeavor to advance shipment and will advise you as soon as the shipment is effected.

We appreciate the business you have secured for us. All further inquiries and orders will continue to receive our prompt and careful attention.

Yours sincerely,

Jeff

Overseas Sales Director

Useful Words & Expressions

I. Widely-used Terms

1. book shipping space	订舱位	2. shipping advice	装运通知
3. P/O(purchase order)	订购单	4. supplementary agreement	补充协议
5. issuing bank	开证行	6. contracted valid period	合同有效期
7. shipping documents	装运单据	8. captioned letter of credit	标题项下的信用证
9. packing list	装箱单	10. Non-negotiable B/Lading	不可转让海运提单
11. advance shipment	提前交货	12. original documents	正本单据
13. negotiating bank	议付行	14. captioned order	标题项下的订单
15. copy documents	副本单据	16. certificate of quality	质量证明书

II. Important Phrases

1. subject goods   标题项下的货物/标的物

2. catch the brisk demand 赶上需求高峰

3. on the way to 在路上

4. schedule to 计划于

5. attached list 附上的清单

6. shipping marks 运输唛头

7. resort to other sources 求助于其它渠道

8. in due time 截止时间

9. prompt action of the shipment 及时装运

10. set out 启程

11. place of origin 原产地

12. go forth 开始

13. on board 装船/在船上

14. place on board the steamer 装到轮船上

15. set forth 阐述

16. best attention 非常重视

17. partial fulfillment 部分履行

18. secure for 达成

III. Expressing Thanks and Purposes of Writing

1. **With reference to** the captioned goods, we are glad to inform you that the relevant L/C was opened yesterday and it is on the way to you.

2. **We are now eager** to know about the shipment of our order No. P/O170802 for 5,000 pieces of imitation jewelry.

3. **With reference to** your letter of August 6th, 2023, urging our prompt action of shipment, we are now glad to inform you that the 5,000 pieces of imitation jewelry have been shipped.

4. **Thank you for your letter dated** August 6th, 2023, asking for definite news of shipment of the subject goods.

5. **Thank you for your order for** the 5,000 pieces of imitation Jewelry.

6. **We have pleasure in informing you that, in accordance with** the stipulations set forth in the captioned letter of credit, today we have shipped the goods on board S.S. "Great Victory" which will sail for your port tomorrow.

IV. Sending Shipping Instructions and Urging an Early Shipment

1. **We have booked shipping space on** S.S. "Great Victory" which is scheduled to sail from

Sete, France to Xingang, Tianjin around the end of next month.

2. Please **get the goods ready for shipment** early.

3. Jewelry is fragile, and **special care should be taken during shipment**.

4. **On the attached list are** particulars of packing and shipping marks, which must be strictly observed.

5. As the selling season is rapidly approaching, our buyers here are **urging us for early delivery**.

6. With this letter, **we wish to draw your attention to the fact that** the L/C will expire at the end of next week and that we are not going to extend it.

7. **Our clients are in urgent need of the goods**, so we cannot afford to wait any longer. Therefore, we will have to resort to other sources of imitation jewelry suppliers if you fail to make the shipment **in due time**.

8. **We shall be very much grateful if you can** effect shipment as soon as possible, thus enabling them to **catch the brisk demand**.

9. **We would like to emphasize that** any delay in shipping our order will undoubtedly involve us in no small difficulty.

10. We believe that all parties involved would definitely **benefit from your prompt action of the shipment.**

11. **Referring to** the subject goods, **we very much regret that** up to now, we have not heard anything about shipment from you about this lot.

12. **We should be glad / Please let us know** when you could manage to ship the goods…

13. **Shipment is to be made in** May / within 3 days / in the first half of March.

It has to be stressed that shipment must be made within the prescribed time limit, as a further extension will not be considered by our end-user.

14. **It is fixed that shipment to be made** before the end of this month and, if possible, we should appreciate your arranging to ship the goods at an earlier date.

15. **We look forward to** your prompt shipment.

The shipment shall be effected as soon as possible.

Immediate delivery would be required.

V. Informing the Shipping Time

1. **The shipment date is approaching**, but we still have not had any news about it since the L/C No. 1708 was issued two weeks ago.

2. The consignment has been on board S.S. "Great Victory", which will set out sailing for your port tomorrow morning.

3. **The shipment is stated with a fixed date**, for example, shipment during January, shipment at/by the end of March, shipment on/before May 15th, shipment during April/May.

4. **An indefinite date of shipment is stipulated** depending on certain conditions such as shipment within 30 days after receipt of L/C, shipment subject to shipping space available, shipment by first available steamer.

5. **The shipment is indicated with a date** in the near future usually in such terms as immediate shipment, prompt shipment, and shipment as soon as possible, but without unified interpretation as to their definite time limit. It is advisable to avoid using these ambiguous terms.

6. **We will ship by** the first steamer available next month.

7. **We are able to effect shipment within** one month after your order has been confirmed.

8. To repack the goods would involve **a delay of about 2 weeks in shipment**.

9. **We inform you with pleasure** that we have booked freight for our Order No.123 on the S.S. … ETD (ETA) … **Please make sure to deliver the goods in time**. For delivery instructions. Please contact… at…

VI. Concerning Shipment Delay

1. **We must apologize for the delay delivery of your order**, which has been caused by the unexpected late arrival of goods from the place of origin.

2. **We are sorry for** not contacting you timely. **We promise to** advise you details of the shipment once the goods are placed on board the steamer.

3. **It is sincerely hoped that** our delay in communicating with you on the above order has caused you no trouble and that shipment will turn out to be completely satisfactory.

4. **We would apologize again for** the inconvenience caused and if there is any loss sustained due to our delay, we will compensate you.

5. **We assure you that** any order from you in the future will get our prompt attention.

6. The goods have long been ready for shipment, but **owing to** the late arrival of your L/C shipment can hardly be effected as anticipated.

7. **We are unable to effect shipment according to** the price and other terms originally agreed upon owing to the delay of your L/C, therefore the responsibility for any loss arising subsequently will wholly rest with you.

8. **We regret that we are unable to** meet your need for advancing the shipment to November.

9. We wish to draw your attention to the fact that the goods have been ready for shipment for a long time and **the covering L/C**, due to arrive here before March 13th, **has not been received up to now**. Please let us know the reason for the delay.

VII. Advising Shipment

1. **We are now glad to inform you that** the 5,000 pieces of imitation jewelry have been shipped.

   We are pleased to inform you that we have booked shipping space for our Order No. … of Chemical Fertilizers on S.S Daching, ETA… For delivery instruction please contact…

2. **To offer more detailed information about the shipment**, tomorrow morning we will fax you the copy of B/L, the original of which is, together with other documents required by the L/C, being passed to you through the negotiating bank and the issuing bank.

3. **We have pleasure in informing you that**, in accordance with the stipulations set forth in the captioned letter of credit, today we have shipped the goods on board S.S. "Great Victory" which will sail for your port tomorrow.

   We have pleasure in advising that we have completed the above shipment according to the stipulations set forth in L/C No…

4. We have airmailed **one set of the shipping documents** covering this deal as follows:
   Our Invoice No. T-F38695 in duplicate
   Packing List No. 89623 in duplicate
   Non-negotiable Bill of Lading No. IJ8769
   Insurance Policy No. TJ0363879
   Certificate of Quality No. TJIJ3865

5. The **original documents** will be sent to you through our bank.
   As for the remaining 1,000 gold plating bracelets and 1,000 anklets, we will endeavor to advance shipment and will advise you as soon as the shipment is effected.

6. **Your order No. … will be shipped by S.S. "Manchester"**.

7. **We advise that/We wish to advise you that…**

8. As per your request we have shipped all your orders by…

9. All your orders booked up to date have been executed.

10. The furs ordered have been dispatched by…

VIII. Expectations for Further Contact

1. **We await your immediate reply.**

We are awaiting your future cooperation.

2. Your early shipping advice will **be highly appreciated**.

3. **We are looking forward to** receiving your shipping advice.

4. **We are pleased that** we have been able to execute your order within the contracted valid period this time and would like to express our strong willingness to pay even more prompt attention to your future orders.

5. **We assure you that** any order from you in the future will get our prompt attention.

6. **We trust** the above shipment will reach you in safe and sound condition and expect to receive your further orders.

7. **We take this opportunity to appreciate** the business between us and **assure** you of our best attention to your future orders.

We appreciate the business you have secured for us.

8. All further inquiries and orders will **continue to receive our prompt and careful attention**.

Exercises

I. Choose the best answer to complete each of the following sentences.

1. It will be appreciated _____ you could effect shipment in two equal lots by the named steamer ship _____ you receive our L/C.

    A. when, when   B. will, soon   C. when, which   D. if, as soon as

2. We will make every _____ to ship the goods as early as possible, and we feel _____ that the shipment will be satisfactory to you in every respect.

    A. effort, sure   B. effect, sure   C. effect, assure   D. effort, assure

3. We have to inform you that, sometimes, transshipment and partial shipment are _____ by the buyer.

    A. permission   B. prohibited   C. permitting   D. allowing

4. We wish to receive your shipping advice as soon as possible for the goods under the captioned _____.

    A. letter   B. contract   C. cable   D. communication

5. We have shipped the captioned goods as required today by the S.S. "Sun" _____ to leave tomorrow.

    A. planned   B. made   C. scheduled   D. decided

6. As the shipment was delayed, the buyer _____ the seller for an explanation.

    A. expedited   B. hastened   C. forced   D. pressed

7. Any omitting or error of the delivery may lead to ____ or even failure in delivery.

    A. inconvenience   B. convenience   C. convenient   D. inconvenient

8. I wonder if you could advance the shipment by half a month ____ we need it urgently.

    A. own to   B. due to   C. because of   D. as

9. The importer will go to the wharf to _____ delivery of the goods.

    A. make   B. effect   C. fulfill   D. take

10. Now the shipment has been arranged to go forth _____ board S.S. "Pigeon", which is scheduled _____ sail for you early next week.

    A. at, on   B. on, on   C. at, to   D. on, to

II. Fill in the blanks with the appropriate words or expressions.

1. We shall be very much _____ if you can _____ shipment as soon as possible, thus enabling them to catch the brisk demand.

2. We have _____ shipping space _____ S.S. "Great Victory" which is _____ to sail from Sete, France to Xingang, Tianjin around the end of next month.

3. We must apologize _____ the delay _____ of your order, which has been caused by the unexpected late arrival of goods from the place of _____.

4. We have _____ in informing you that, in accordance _____ the stipulations set forth in the captioned letter of credit, today we have _____ the goods on board S.S. "Great Victory".

5. We trust the above shipment will _____ you in safe and sound _____ and expect to receive your further orders.

III. Give the English/Chinese equivalents of the following expressions.

1. 转运 _____
2. 装船通知 _____
3. 装船指示 _____
4. 及时装运 _____
5. 舱位 _____
6. 直达轮 _____
7. 标题项下的合同 _____
8. consignment note _____
9. effect shipment _____
10. fulfill one's obligation _____

11. deliver the goods _____   12. load the goods _____

13. ocean transportation _____   14. partial shipment _____

IV. Translate the following sentences into English/Chinese.

1. 装运期的任何延误都会增加货物的储存费用。

2. 我们尽快通知你们装船日期。

3. 按你方要求，兹随函附寄一整套的装船单据包括商业发票、装箱单和已装船清洁提单。所有单据均一式三份。

4. We wish to draw your attention to the fact that the shipment is approaching, but nothing has been received from you about its shipment under the captioned contract.

5. We have pleasure in informing you that, in accordance with the stipulations set forth in the captioned letter of credit, today we have shipped the goods on board S.S. "Great Victory" which will sail for your port tomorrow.

V. Complete the gaps with the appropriate words.

Letter 1

Dear Denny,

We are now eager to know about the __1__ of our order No. 170802 for 5,000 pieces of imitation jewelry. The shipment date is __2__, but we still have not had any news about it since the __3__ No. 1708 was __4__ two weeks ago.

With this letter, we wish to call your attention to the fact that the L/C will __5__ at the end of next week and that we are not going to __6__ it. And our clients are in urgent need of the goods, so we cannot __7__ to wait any longer. Therefore, we will have to resort to other sources of imitation jewelry suppliers if you fail to make the shipment in the __8__ time.

We believe that all parties involved would definitely __9__ from your prompt action of the shipment. We are looking forward to receiving your shipping __10__.

Yours sincerely,

×××

Letter 2

Dear Sirs,

We have pleasure in __1__ you that we have completed the above shipment in accordance with the __2__ set forth in the captioned Letter of Credit, and we __3__ our fax of today's date, reading:

"S/C NO. 1821 L/C NO. 1804 4,000 DOZEN SHIRTS SHIPPED PEACE SAILING 001"

We are sending you under cover one set of duplicate shipping __4__ so that you may make all the necessary preparations to take __5__ of the goods, when they duly arrive at your port.

Our Invoice No. 1802 in __6__

Packing __7__ No. 1809 in duplicate

Non-negotiable Bill of __8__ No. AD1810

Insurance Policy No. BG1811

We trust the above shipment will __9__ you in sound condition and expect to receive your further __10__ before long.

We look forward to your early reply.

Yours faithfully,
× × ×

VI. Translate the following letter into Chinese.

Dear Sirs,

With reference to your letter dated March 25th, we regret that we are not able to ship the captioned goods as required.

Since the selling season is approaching, we are heavily committed at present. We can hardly get the whole lot ready within half a month. Also, we have contacted the shipping company and been told that there is no shipping space available on ships sailing from here to your port before April 15th, and the shipping space has been fully booked up to the end of next month. So we would suggest that you allow us to ship the half of the goods via Hong Kong, which will not result in any delay in your receiving the goods if you confirm at your earliest convenience.

Thank you in advance for your kind cooperation.

Yours faithfully,
× × ×

VII. Writing.

1. You, Brad, placed an order for 3,000 electronic calculators, requiring shipment not later

than November 30th. But, you have not had any information about the shipment up till now and you write to your exporter, Dennis, urging a punctual shipment. In your letter you give reasons for urging shipment and state the consequence.

2. You, George, write a letter to inform Hunk of the shipment of his order No. HD5689. The goods will be shipped ex S.S. Princess, sailing for Shanghai on November 15th, and the ETA may be December 20th. In your letter, you also refer to drawing upon Hunk a sight L/C as stipulated in the S/C.

 微课视频

扫一扫，获取本课相关微课视频。

9.1.1　Case Study.mp4

9.1.2　Relevant Information.mp4

9.1.3　Writing Skills.mp4

9.2.1　Letter 1 Sending Shipping Instructions.mp4

9.2.2　Letter 2 Urging an Early Shipment.mp4

9.2.3　Letter 4 Delay Shipment.mp4

9.2.4　Letter 5 Shipping Advice.mp4

Unit 10　Insurance

10.1　Background Knowledge

10.1.1　Case Study

1. Case One

You are an exporter of toys. Suppose that you are exchanging information about insurance of two transactions with your partner. One transaction is based on CIF term and the other is under FOB term. What are the essential differences of your information exchange between these two transactions?

2. Case Two

Suppose you are Eddie. You receive the following letter. Please share your answers to the following questions: Why does the seller write this letter? What core information does the writer hope to convey to the recipient?

To: "Eddie Lake" <johnghinc@gmail.com>   **From:** "Gavin Cliff" <smithsontradecompany@hotmail.com>   **Subject:** Your Order No. 1708, Our S/C No. 708 Covering 3,000 Toys
Dear Eddie,   Thank you for your letter of July 30th, requesting us to effect insurance on the captioned shipment for your account.

We are pleased to inform you that we have covered the above shipment with the People's Insurance Company of China against All Risks for $9,900. The policy will be sent to you in a day or two together with our debit note for the premium.

For your information, this order will be shipped on S.S. "East Wind", sailing on or about August 20th.

Best regards,

Yours faithfully,

Gavin

Sales Manager

10.1.2　Relevant Information

In international business, goods have to be transported from the consignor in one country to the consignee in another country far away. During transit, the transportation of the goods has to go through the procedures of loading, unloading, storing, etc. This process involves various risks, which may result in the damage to or loss of the goods. To protect the goods against the possible losses, before shipment, the buyer or the seller applies to an insurance company for insurance covering the goods to be transported. There are mainly four types of insurance coverage: marine insurance, air insurance, land insurance and postal insurance. As far as foreign trade is concerned, marine insurance is the most important. So, this unit discusses this type and the relevant business letters.

There are many insurance companies in the world. The Lloyd's Insurance Company, London is a famous organization incorporated in London in 1871. The People's Insurance Company of China (PICC) established in 1949, is the only state-owned insurance organization in China, which has made great contribution to the protection of China's export/import from perils and loss.

1. Types of Marine Cargo Insurance

In China's international trade, the People's Insurance Company of China (PICC) enjoys high prestige in setting claims promptly and equitably. PICC has its own insurance clauses known as

China Insurance Clauses (CIC). According to its Ocean Marine Cargo Clauses, the basic marine policy covers basic risks and additional risks.

(1) Basic Risks include Free from Particular Average (FPA), With Particular Average (WPA/WA) and All Risks (AR).

(2) Additional Risks, covering losses by Extraneous Risks, are divided into General Additional Risks and Special Additional Risks.

All Risks is the most commonly used type of risks. To insure All Risks is of most convenience just because it covers FPA, WPA and 11 kinds of general additional risks. The insured need not care what kinds of additional risks to choose. Nevertheless, the most convenient service will have to pay the maximum cost.

2. Insurance Amount

Generally speaking, the insurance amount is defined as 110% of the total invoice value, that is, the total value of the goods based on CIF price plus 10% of it. Under CIF term, if the importer requires more than 110% of the total value, the importer has to bear the additional premium.

Insurance is covered by the buyer or the seller in conformity with the terms of sales contract. Whoever takes out the insurance should be familiar with the following formula:

Insurance Amount=CIF×110%

Insurance Premium=Insurance Amount×Premium Rate

3. Insurance Documents

The most common insurance documents include insurance policy, insurance certificate, open policy, etc. These insurance documents, though named differently, are almost of the same legal force and form the part of the shipping documents. Insurance policy is the most detailed and official among them. As part of the shipping documents, insurance document contains all the details concerning the goods, coverage, premium and the insurance amount and serves as evidence of the agreement between the insurer and the party taking out insurance. The risks covered under the policy should be strictly in accordance with the terms of the contract and with those of the letter of credit, if the shipment is made under it.

4. Insurance Claim

An insurance claim, if any, should be submitted to the insurance company or its agent as soon as possible so as to provide the latter with enough time to pursue recovery from the relative party in fault. When the insured lodges an insurance claim the following documents are to be presented:

insurance policy or certificate, bill of lading, commercial invoice, survey report, master's protest and statement of claim for processing.

5. Selecting the Suitable Insurance Coverage

When buying insurance, one has to know what risks can be covered and to decide how much coverage is needed so as to obtain as much protection as necessary at as low a cost as possible. Here are the four essential points to refer to for selecting insurance coverage:

(1) Type, nature and characteristics and packing of the goods;

(2) Transportation of the goods, including partial shipment and transshipment to be allowed or not, the condition of the vessel, the voyage line, etc.;

(3) The damage and/or loss may occur at ports and in the process of loading and unloading in transit;

(4) Social and political situation of the places and countries which the goods have to pass by and reach.

10.1.3　Writing Skills

1. Writing Skills of Letters about Insurance Coverage for the Goods

As people say, without insurance, there would not be modern international trade. To select the suitable coverage is very important. The two parties contact each other to negotiate the matter. When writing such letters, the writers are recommended to follow these skills:

(1) Relevance: Refer to the relevant goods to be covered and the shipment to be made with related document numbers, such as the order, the contract, or the L/C, if any, for the recipient's reference to and reminding of the transaction.

(2) Completeness: Provide the details of the insurance coverage to be selected, including the insurance company, the type of coverage, the insurance amount, the premium rate, the duration, etc.

(3) Conciseness: State your opinion clearly and briefly, focusing on the subject of selecting the suitable insurance coverage. Don't scatter information to distract the recipient.

2. Writing Skills of Letters about Asking to Amend Insurance Clause

If the buyer finds the insurance clause in the Sales Contract unacceptable or inappropriate, he will contact the seller, requiring amending the insurance clause. To write such a letter, the buyer is often recommended to observe the following writing skills:

(1) Directness: Put forward the problem directly and clearly at the beginning of the letter, quoting the unacceptable original clause and stating your amending requirements;

(2) Profession: Give professional amending requirements and rational explanations, making your amendments professional, reasonable and acceptable;

(3) Courtesy: Use courteous words to give your requirements and express thanks for cooperation and expectations for early replies with a sincere and friendly tone.

3. Writing Skills of Letters about Excessive Insurance Coverage

In trade practice, sometimes, the buyer may ask the seller to take out excessive insurance coverage on the buyer's behalf. To write such a letter well, the buyer is often advised to take the following writing skills:

(1) Courtesy: Express your thanks for the cooperation at the very beginning and your expectations for approval in the close of the letter with courteous words and friendly tone.

(2) Reasonability: Give reasonable requirements and acceptable explanations, making sure that your requirements are based on professional knowledge and related rules and regulations.

(3) Conciseness: Refer to the important relevant document, such as the S/C, the order or the L/C, as the reference, and then give your specific requirements. When the necessary information is provided, bring the letter to an end.

10.2 Sample Letters and Basic Writing Structure Analysis

In letters of insurance, importers and exporters mainly talk about the following points: insurance coverage, insurance requirements, insurance clause, insurance amount, insurance premium, etc.

10.2.1 Basic Writing Structures of Letters Concerning the Coverage

In international trade, for the insurance of the goods, the two parties will discuss coverage in details. Generally, such letters include the following parts:

1. The relevant goods and shipment information with related document number for reference;
2. The details about the coverage of insurance;
3. The hope for a timely reply.

Letter 1　Talking about the Coverage Adopted for the Goods

To: "Kris"<pondcatradeinc@gmail.com>
From: "Amanda" <everydecorationscoltd@hotmail.com>
Subject: Your Order No. D/P170682 for 5,000 Pieces Glass Accessories

Dear Kris,

Please be informed that we will be shipping your Order No. D/P170682 for 5,000 pieces of glass accessories per S.S. "Changyuan" due to leave Ningbo at the end of this month or the beginning of next month.

Unless otherwise instructed, we will arrange to effect an All Risk insurance for you on the captioned cargo. This type of coverage is, in our opinion, necessary for a cargo of this nature.

Your early reply will be highly appreciated.

Yours sincerely,

Amanda Zhao

Overseas Sales Director

10.2.2　Basic Writing Structures of Letters Concerning Excessive Insurance Coverage

　　Sometimes, considering the nature of the goods, the buyer hopes to cover them for excessive insurance, he/she will ask the seller to do the job on his/her behalf. Such a letter often includes the following points:

　　1. Refer to the relevant goods and the document number;

　　2. Ask for extra insurance you desire and promise to pay the extra premium;

　　3. Expect for the acceptance.

Letter 2 Talking about Excessive Insurance Coverage

To: "Amanda" <everydecorationscoltd@hotmail.com>
From: "Kris" <pondcatradeinc@gmail.com>
Subject: Our Order No. D/P170682 for 5,000 Pieces Glass Accessories

Dear Amanda,

We wish to refer you to our Order No. D/P170682 for 5,000 pieces of glass accessories which are placed on CIF basis.

In accordance with the Contract No. AK17062, you are requested to insure the goods against All Risks at invoice value plus 10%. But now we desire to have the shipment insured for 130% of the invoice value. The extra premium will be for our account.

We sincerely hope that our request will not bring much trouble to you. We await your shipping advice.

Yours sincerely,

Kris Wood

Overseas Purchasing Director

10.2.3 Basic Writing Structures of Letters Concerning Asking the Seller to Cover Insurance

If a transaction is concluded on FOB or CFR, etc., the seller will not hold his/her responsibility for insurance coverage of the goods. In this case, the buyer may ask the seller to make insurance on his/her behalf. The buyer's letter should contain the following points:

    1. Refer to the order number and the exact business terms adopted;
    2. Give your request for insurance, including the type of insurance and the insurance rate, etc.;
    3. State clearly how the premium will be paid;
    4. Expect for an acceptance.

Letter 3　Asking the Seller to Effect Insurance

To: "Debbie" <woodklfoodcompany@gmail.com>
From: "Emily" <sunnynutritiousfoodinc@gmail.com>
Subject: Our Order No. 9678 for 500 Cartons of Canned Mushroom

Dear Debbie,

We would like you to refer to our Order No. 9678 for 500 cartons of canned mushroom from which you will see that this order was placed on CFR basis.

As now we wish to have the captioned goods insured at your end, we shall be much obliged if you will arrange insurance on our behalf against W.P.A., T.P.N.D, Clash & Breakage Risks and War Risk for 110% of the invoice value, i.e. USD38,500, with the People's Insurance Company of China.

We shall, of course, refund the premium to you on receipt of your debit note and the covering insurance policy.

We sincerely hope that our request will meet with your approval.

Yours sincerely,

Emily

Overseas Purchasing Director

After receiving Emily's letter, Debbie accepted the requirement and wrote a letter in reply. Her letter includes the following structure:

1. Confirm the receipt of the letter;
2. Inform the recipient of the relative insurance information;
3. Advise shipment.

Letter 4 A Reply to the Letter Above

To: "Emily" <sunnynutritiousfoodinc@gmail.com>
From: "Debbie" <woodklfoodcompany@gmail.com>
Subject: Your Order No. 9678 for 500 Cartons of Canned Mushroom

Dear Emily,

This is to acknowledge receipt of your letter dated July 28th requesting us to effect insurance on the captioned shipment for your account.

We are pleased to inform you that we have covered the above shipment with the People's Insurance Company of China against W.P.A., T.P.N.D, Clash & Breakage Risks and War Risk for USD 38,500. The policy is being prepared accordingly and will be forwarded to you by the end of the week together with our debit note for the premium.

For your information, we are making arrangements to ship the 500 cartons of canned mushroom by S.S. "White Cloud", sailing on or about August 15th.

Yours sincerely,

Debbie

Overseas Sales Director

10.2.4 Basic Writing Structures of Letters Concerning Insurance Clause

In international trade, if the buyer can't accept the insurance clause in the Sales Contract, the two parties will negotiate insurance clause. Usually, the buyer writes to the seller, requiring amending the insurance clause. Such letters should contain the following points:

1. Point out the problem directly and clearly;
2. Give your request for insurance, and explain the reasons;
3. Expect for an acceptance.

Letter 5　Asking to Amend Insurance Clause

To: "Allen" <parkinsonwoodinc@gmail.com>
From: "Dennis" <hqpotteryandporcelaintradecompany@hotmail.com>
Subject: Your S/C No. 17083

Dear Allen,

With reference to your Sales Confirmation No. 17083, we regret to point out that the insurance clause in your S/C, saying "The insurance is to be covered on the goods for 110% of the insurance value against W.P.A and Breakage", is unacceptable to us.

As porcelain wares are delicate goods and are likely to be damaged on the voyage, W.P.A & Breakage will not be good enough. Therefore, we have to ask for broader coverage. Please take out coverage on our cargo against Hook Damage Risk, W.P.A. and Breakage Risks.

We shall be grateful if you can amend your S/C. We sincerely hope for a favorable reply from you.

Yours sincerely,

Dennis

Overseas Purchasing Manager

In such circumstances, the seller's reply should include the following parts:

1. Confirm the receipt of the letter and state your usual practice;
2. Give your response to the problem: accept or refuse, and your requirements or reasons;
3. Hope for an early reply.

Letter 6　A Reply to the Letter Above

To: "Dennis" <hqpotteryandporcelaintradecompany@hotmail.com>
From: "Allen" <parkinsonwoodinc@gmail.com>
Subject: Insurance Clause

Dear Dennis,

In reply to your letter of July 16th, requiring us to amend the S/C No. 17083 concerning insurance clause covering the consignment of porcelain wares, we would like to advise you that according to our usual practice, we cover this cargo sold on CIF terms for 110% of the insurance value against W.P.A and Breakage in the absence of definite instructions from our clients.

If you want to take out coverage on your cargo against Hook Damage Risk and T.P.N.D. in addition to W.P.A. & Breakage Risks, we can arrange it for you with a slightly higher premium. The extra premium will be at your expense.

We hope that everything is clear to you and look forward to your early reply.

Yours sincerely,

Allen

Overseas Sales Director

Useful Words & Expressions

I. Widely-used Terms

1. effect insurance — 投保
2. All Risks — 一切险
3. policy — 保险单
4. debit note — 借记单
5. premium — 保险费
6. coverage — 保险覆盖的范围
7. W.P.A — 水渍险
8. T.P.N.D — 偷窃提货不着险
9. War Risk — 战争险
10. Clash & Breakage Risks — 碰损、破碎险
11. insurance clause — 保险条款
12. insurance value — 保险金额
13. Hook Damage Risk — 钩损险

II. Important Phrases

1. captioned shipment — 标题项下装运的货物
2. for one's account — 由某人支付

3. for one's information   供某人参考

4. due to   就要

5. unless otherwise instructed   除非另有指示

6. captioned cargo   标题下的货物

7. cargo of this nature   货物的属性

8. placed on CIF basis   根据 CIF 下的订单

9. insure the goods   给货物投保

10. shipment insured   给运输的货物投保

11. covering insurance policy   相关保险单

12. this is to acknowledge receipt of   确认收到

13. delicate goods   易碎的货物

14. broader coverage   扩大保险险种

15. take out coverage   负责投保

16. in the absence of   在没有……的情况下

17. at one's expense   由某人支付

III. Insurance

1. insurance on the 100 tons of wool

2. insurance against all risks

3. insurance for 110% of the invoice value

4. insurance at a slightly higher premium

5. insurance at the rate of 5‰

6. insurance with the People's Insurance Company of China

IV. Purpose of Writing (Providing Detailed Relevant Information)

1. **Please be informed that we will be shipping your Order** No. D/P170682 for 5,000 pieces glass accessories per S.S. Changyuan due to leave Ningbo at the end of this month or the beginning of next month.

2. **We wish to refer you to our Order** No. D/P170682 for 5,000 pieces of glass accessories which are placed on CIF basis.

3. **We would like you to refer to our Order** No. 9678 for 500 cartons of canned mushroom from which you will see that this order was placed on CFR basis.

4. **This is to acknowledge the receipt of your letter dated** July 28th requesting us to effect

insurance on the captioned shipment for your account.

5. **With reference to your Sales Confirmation** No. 17083, we regret to point out that the insurance clause in your S/C, saying "The insurance is to be covered on the goods for 110% of the insurance value against W.P.A and Breakage", is unacceptable to us.

6. **In reply to your letter** of July 16th, requiring us to amend the S/C No. 17083 concerning…

V. Concerning/Negotiating Detailed Insurance Coverage

1. **We are pleased to confirm** having **covered** the above shipment with the People's Insurance Company of China against All Risks for $9,900.

The policy will be sent to you in a day or two **together with** our debit note for the premium.

2. **We have covered insurance** on the 100 metric tons of wool for 110% of the invoice value against All Risks.

In the absence of definite instructions from our clients, we generally **cover insurance against** W.P.A and War Risk; if you desire to cover F.P.A.(Free from Particular Average), please let us know in advance.

For transactions concluded on CIF basis, we usually **cover the insurance against** All Risks at invoice value plus 10% with the People's Insurance Company of China as per CIC of January 1st.

We can **cover all basic risks** as required as long as they are stipulated in the Ocean Marine Cargo Clauses of the Lloyd's Insurance Company, London.

Please see that the above mentioned goods should be **covered** for 150% of invoice value against All Risks. We know that according to your usual practice, you insure the goods only for 10% above invoice value; therefore the extra premium will be for our account.

3. Unless otherwise instructed, we will arrange to **effect an All Risk insurance** for you on the captioned cargo. This type of coverage is, in our opinion, necessary for a cargo of this nature.

We will **effect insurance against the usual risks**, for the value of the goods plus freight.

We will **effect insurance against all risks**, charging premium and freight to the consignments.

4. **In accordance with** the Contract No. AK17062, **you are requested to insure** the goods against All Risks at invoice value plus 10%.

But now we desire to have the shipment insured for 130% of the invoice value.

The extra premium will be for our account.

5. As now **we wish to have the captioned goods insured at your end**, we shall be much obliged if you will **arrange insurance on our behalf against** W.P.A., T.P.N.D, Clash & Breakage

Risks and War Risk for 110% of the invoice value, i.e. USD38,500, with the **People's Insurance Company of China**.

6. We shall of course refund the premium to you on receipt of your debit note and **the covering insurance policy.**

7. We are pleased to inform you that **we have covered the above shipment with the People's Insurance Company of China against** W.P.A., T.P.N.D, Clash & Breakage Risks and War Risk for USD 38,500. The policy is being prepared accordingly and will be forwarded to you by the end of the week together with our debit note for the premium.

8. **For your information, this order will be shipped on** S.S. "East Wind", sailing on or about August 20.

For your information, we are making arrangements to ship the 500 cartons of canned mushroom by S.S. "White Cloud", sailing on or about August 15th.

9. **Will you please quote us a rate for the insurance against all risks of a shipment** of… from… to… by S.S. … The invoice value is…

10. **We are making regular shipments from… to…** and should be glad to hear whether you would be prepared to issue an open policy.

11. As you will be placing regular orders with us, we suggest that we **take out an open policy for** approximately $1,500,000 annually. **The rate for insurance would be** 46 percent, and would cover all risks except war, warehouse to warehouse, on scheduled sailings.

12. **Please insure/cover us** on the cargo listed on the attached sheet.

13. **I regret to report the loss of… insured with you under the above policy**.

VI. Negotiating/Discussing Detailed Insurance Clause

Reasons for Amending the Insurance Clause

1. **With reference to** your Sales Confirmation No. 17083, we regret to point out that **the insurance clause** in your S/C, saying "**The insurance is to be covered** on the goods for 110% of **the insurance value against** W.P.A and Breakage", is **unacceptable** to us.

2. **As** porcelain wares are delicate goods and are likely to be damaged on the voyage, W.P.A & Breakage will not be good enough.

Therefore, **we have to ask for** broader coverage.

3. **Please take out coverage on our cargo against** Hook Damage Risk, W.P.A. **and** Breakage Risks.

4. We shall be grateful if you can **amend your S/C.**

Unit 10   Insurance

Accepting/Refusing the Amending Requirements

1. **In reply to your letter of** July 16th requiring us to amend the S/C No. 17083 concerning insurance clause covering the consignment of porcelain wares, **we would like to advise you that** according to our usual practice, **we cover this cargo** sold on CIF terms **for 110% of the insurance value against** W.P.A. and Breakage in the absence of definite instructions from our clients.

2. **If you want to take out coverage on your cargo against** Hook Damage Risk and T.P.N.D. in addition to W.P.A. & Breakage Risks, **we can arrange it for you** with a slightly higher premium. The extra premium will be **at your expense**.

3. **Owing to the fact that** these bags have occasionally been **dropped into the water** during loading and unloading, the insurers have raised the premium to…%. We are therefore of the opinion that **it would be to your advantage to have** W.A. (With Average / With Particular Average) cover **instead of** F.P.A.

Owing to the risk of war, **we cannot accept the insurance** at the ordinary rate. At the same time, **it would be to your advantage to have** particular average **cover**.

VII. Expectations for Further Contact

1. Your early reply will **be highly appreciated**.

2. **We sincerely hope that** our request will not bring much trouble to you.

We sincerely hope that our request will meet with your approval.

We sincerely hope for a favorable reply from you.

3. **We await** your shipping advice.

4. **We hope that** everything is clear to you and look forward to your early reply.

5. As you hold the policy, **we should be grateful if you** would take the matter up for us with the underwriters to ensure indemnification.

Exercises

I. Choose the best answer to complete each of the following sentences.

1. In accordance with the Contract No. 1805, you are requested to insure the goods _____ All Risks _____ invoice value plus 10%.

  A. for, on   B. under, with   C. against, at   D. by, under

2. Complying with your request, we shall insure _____ F.P.A. (or W.P.A) on the above goods.

  A. /   B. for   C. against   D. with

3. As requested, we have covered insurance _____ 5,000 glass accessories per S.S. Dongfang _____ 10% above the invoice value for All Risks.

  A. with, on B. on, at C. for, with D. against, under

4. With reference to your Sales Confirmation No. 18099, we regret to point out that you are not allowed to insure the goods _____ 150% _____ invoice value.

  A. for, of B. at, of C. against, under D. for, with

5. Unless otherwise instructed, we will arrange to _____ an All Risk insurance for you on the captioned cargo.

  A. buy B. effect C. have D. afford

6. We shall of course _____ the premium to you on receipt of your debit note and the covering insurance policy.

  A. give B. provide C. offer D. refund

7. You could inform us of the full details regarding insurance _____ handled by the People's Insurance Company of China for our reference.

  A. coverage B. range C. limits D. scope

8. However, we are regretful to say that we wish to point out the extra premium is _____.

  A. under your account B. at your account

  C. for your account D. on your account

9. This _____ is to be covered under our "open-cover" terms.

  A. goods B. consignment C. lot D. insurance

10. Unless we hear from you _____ the contrary before the end of this month, we shall arrange to cover the goods against F.P.A. for the value of the goods plus freight.

  A. on B. above C. to D. in

II. Fill in the blanks with the appropriate words or expressions.

1. But now we desire to have the shipment insured _____ 130% _____ the invoice value. The extra premium will be _____ our account.

2. As now we wish to have the captioned goods _____ at your end, we shall be much obliged if you will _____ insurance on our behalf _____ W.P.A.

3. We have _____ insurance _____ the 500 sets "Lenovo" Brand computers _____ 110% of the invoice value against all risks _____ the People's Insurance Company of China.

4. As porcelain wares are _____ goods and likely to be _____ on the voyage, W.P.A & Breakage will not be good enough.

5. The insurance _____ is being prepared accordingly and will be _____ to you by the end of the week together with our debit _____ for the premium.

III. Give the English/Chinese equivalents of the following expressions.

1. 保一切险 _____
2. 平安险 _____
3. 额外保费 _____
4. 淡水雨淋险 _____
5. 保单 _____
6. 渗漏险 _____
7. 串味险 _____
8. 短缺险 _____
9. 保额 _____
10. T.P.N.D. (Theft, Pilferage & Non-delivery) _____
11. W.A. / W.P.A. (With Average or With Particular Average) _____
12. 110% of invoice value _____
13. Risk of Intermixture and Contamination _____
14. Strikes Risk _____

IV. Translate the following sentences into English/Chinese.

1. 我们已将 5 000 台空调按发票金额的 110%投保一切险。

2. 如果买方要求附加险，额外保险费由买方承担。

3. 如果没有你们的明确指示，我们将按一般惯例投水渍险和战争险。

4. We generally insure our export shipments with the People's Insurance Company of China.

5. The policy holder may, within 30 days of any loss or damage to the property insured, file a claim with the insurance company.

V. Complete the gaps with the appropriate words.

Letter 1

Dear Sirs,

    This is to __1__ receipt of your letter dated May 19th requiring us to amend the S/C No. 18099 concerning insurance clause __2__ the ceramic vases. We would like to advise you that according to our usual practice, we cover this cargo sold __3__ CIF terms __4__ 110% of the insurance value __5__ W.P.A. and Breakage in the absence of definite instructions from our clients.

    We regret to inform you that if you want to take out __6__ on your cargo against Hook Damage Risk and T.P.N.D. in __7__ to W.P.A. & Breakage Risks, we can __8__ it for you with a slightly higher __9__. The extra premium will be at your __10__.

We hope that everything is clear to you and look forward to your early reply.

Yours sincerely,

×××

Letter 2

Dear Sirs,

We are the __1__ of the Insurance Policy No. 1809 __2__ by your company on 5,000kgs of Chemical Fertilizer __3__ by S.S. "Sunrise". We regret to __4__ you that during the voyage the ship encountered bad weather and the above consignment incurred heavy __5__. We have arranged __6__ the surveyor to investigate the extent of the __7__ and shall forward his report together with our claim as soon as possible.

As required, the underwriters are responsible for the claim as far as it is within the scope of __8__, so please let us know what __9__ you need from us when we submit our __10__.

Yours faithfully,

×××

VI. Translate the following letter into Chinese.

Dear Sirs,

Re: Insurance

We are in receipt of your letter of February 15th, quoting us for 300 boxes of Electronic Toy Cars on CIF terms. However, we are regretful to say that we prefer to have your quotation on CFR terms.

For your reference, we have taken out an open policy with the People's Insurance Company of China, which is a state-operated enterprise with high reputation and its agents in all main ports and regions of the world. Should any damage occur to the goods, their agent at your end will take up the matter without delay. Besides, we have a long-term cooperation. The underwriters usually give us a handsome premium rebate at regular intervals.

We look forward to receiving your early reply.

Yours faithfully,

×××

VII. Writing

1. You are Mason, an exporter of glassware. Your trade partner, Kris Baker, ordering 300 cases pottery with you, wrote you a letter on August 10th, requesting you to effect insurance for his account against All Risks for USD3,000. You make insurance with the People's Insurance Company of China as required and write a reply letter to Mason, notifying the covering of insurance and also mentioning the arrangement of shipment.

2. You, Jerry, bought some cotton cloths amounting to GBP30,000 from Raymond Huang and now you are writing a letter to give your request for insurance. In your letter, first you refer to the opening of the confirmed, irrevocable L/C No. 3269 amounting to GBP30,000 with validity until October 31th through the Bank of China. Then you give your requirement for All Risks for 110% of the invoice value. Finally, you express your expectation for an early shipping advice.

 微课视频

扫一扫，获取本课相关微课视频。

10.1.1　Case Study.mp4

10.1.2　Relevant Information.mp4

10.1.3　Writing Skills.mp4

10.2.1　Letter 1 Talking about the Coverage Adopted for the Goods.mp4

10.2.2　Letter 2 Talking about Excessive Insurance Coverage.mp4

10.2.3　Letter 3 Asking the Seller to Effect Insurance.mp4

10.2.4　Letter 5 Asking to Amend Insurance Clause.mp4

Unit 11　Complaints and Adjustments

11.1　Background Knowledge

11.1.1　Case Study

1. Case One

Golden Star Co., Ltd. has placed an order with DGM Co., Ltd. for B/O toys on January 5th. However, after the arrival of the goods, Golden Star Co., Ltd. has found the packages broken and the toys in the open. To claim for the loss, Golden Star Co., Ltd. lodges a complaint to DGM Co., Ltd. and asks them to make up the losses.

To: "Wilson"<botoystradeinc@gmail.com>
From: "Richard Selzer" <hellokidscoltd@hotmail.com>
Subject: Compensation for the Loss of Improper Packing

Dear Wilson,

　　The B/O toys you shipped per S.S. "Peace" on March 2nd arrived here yesterday.
　　On examination, nearly 20% of the packages had been broken and the toys were in pieces. It was obviously attributed to improper packing.
　　We are, therefore, compelled to claim on you to compensate us for the loss, $1,000, which we have sustained by the damage to the goods. We should like to take this opportunity to suggest that special care be taken in your future deliveries.
　　We hope we can get a satisfactory answer within one week. We are waiting for your early

> reply.
>
> Yours faithfully,
> Richard Selzer

2. Case Two

Write a letter of claim for inferior quality regarding the following contents: The consignment on S.S. "Peace" under S/C K9308 was found some cases badly damaged. The Survey Report issued by Xiamen Commodity Inspection Bureau is sent to you and we hope that you will lodge a claim against the relevant Insurance Company on our behalf.

11.1.2 Relevant Information

1. Definitions of a Complaint and a Claim

In international business, a complaint usually refers to an expression of dissatisfaction made to a responsible party. In business letter writing, when one party makes a complaint, he/she usually provides evidences or documentation about a problem with a product or service.

In international business, a claim is usually a demand made by one party to another for a certain amount of compensation on account of loss and/or damage sustained through its negligence.

The purpose of writing a letter of complaint or claim is to get better service or reasonable compensation instead of accusing the others. Accusations do not help either company. They often make it more difficult to correct the errors and to work together in the future. Thus, a complaint letter to a supplier, customer, or other businessperson about their work must be written in a restrained and tactful way.

2. Reasons for Claims

In international trade, claims are often made for such reasons as follows: loss or shortage of the goods; not opening an L/C in time; delayed shipment; quality discrepancy; wrong delivery; inferior quality; insufficient packing; delay in payment.

3. Points for Attention in Complaining

There are some points for attention in complaining.

(1) For international shipment, any claim by the buyer shall reach the seller within 21 days after the arrival of the goods at the destination stated in B/L accompanied with satisfactory

evidence thereof.

(2) For domestic shipment, any claim by the buyer shall be posted within 30 days after the arrival of the goods at the place of the end-user.

(3) The seller shall not be responsible for damages that may result from the use of goods.

(4) The seller shall not be responsible for any amount in excess of the invoice value of the defective goods.

11.1.3 Writing Skills

1. Writing Skills for Lodging a Complaint or Claim

If the goods are found damaged or lost upon arrival, the consignee should preserve the spot and the original state of the cargo, then immediately notify the insurer or its agent for a joint survey. With the survey report, the consignee can lodge a complaint or claim to the party concerned. To lodge a complaint or claim, the following principles may help you:

(1) Timeliness: When the goods are found damaged or lost upon arrival, file a complaint or claim to the party concerned immediately.

(2) Courtesy: No matter how aggravating the circumstances are, you should always write courteously as this style of writing fosters a positive relationship with your reader and is more likely to bring about a favorable response. You'd better address your readers politely, use positive words and phrases, and stress what can be done.

(3) Clarity and concreteness: You should explain the problems clearly and objectively. Using concrete expressions to make a specific request so that your readers know exactly what is required or desired.

2. Writing Skills for Dealing with a Claim

When receiving a complaint, try to answer promptly to show your sincerity. The following skills may help you in dealing with a claim:

(1) Adopting a "you" attitude: You need to recognize and understand the claimant's situation and you should be willing to solve the problems, if any. Even if there is nothing for your business, when you receive a claim, you should deal with it in a sincere and courteous way. Please don't deny it at the first glance or simply ignore it.

(2) Conciseness: There is no need for the sellers to go into a long story of how the mistakes were made. A short explanation may be useful, but generally speaking, the buyers are not interested in hearing how or why the error occurred but only in having the matter put right, in receiving the goods they ordered — or at least the value for the money they have paid — or in knowing when they may expect to receive the delayed consignment.

(3) Sincerity: To assure your customer that his/her complaint has been seriously considered, you can use facts to convince him/her of your position.

11.2　Sample Letters and Basic Writing Structure Analysis

11.2.1　Basic Writing Structures of Letters Concerning Complaints or Claims

As mentioned above, complaint in international trade is an expression of dissatisfaction with a product or service, either orally or in writing, from the customer. Effective complaint letters (and any other ways of complaining) should be concise, authoritative, factual, constructive and friendly. To write an effective complaint letter, the buyer should make sure the letter arranged in such a way as follows:

1. Begin by regretting the need to complain and mention the date of the order, the date of delivery and the goods complained about.

2. In the body part, give additional or detailed information about why it is necessary to write this letter, why and how you are inconvenienced, etc., in order to state your reasons for being dissatisfied and ask for an explanation.

3. Suggest how the matter should be put right, substitute the right merchandise for the wrong ones, improve the service, correct the bill, etc.

4. Close the letter courteously with a request for prompt action.

Letter 1　Buyer's Claim for Short Weight

To: "David Choi" <forevertradeinc@gmail.com> **From:** "J. Wong" <wondertoyscoltd@hotmail.com> **Subject:** Order No. 768197
Dear Mr. David Choi, 　　I am writing to inform you that the goods we ordered from your company have not been supplied correctly. 　　On May 17th, 2024 we placed an order with your firm for 12,000 R/C toys. The consignment

arrived yesterday but it contained only 1,200 R/C toys.

This error put our firm in a difficult position, as we had to make some emergency purchases to fulfill our commitments to all our customers. This caused us considerable inconvenience.

Please make up the shortfall immediately and ensure that such errors will not be made again. Otherwise, we may have to look elsewhere for our supplies.

I look forward to hearing from you.

Yours sincerely,

J. Wong

Purchasing Officer

Letter 2   Buyer's Complaint for Improper Packing

To: "Jones" <curetoyscoltd@hotmail.com>
From: "David" <forevertradeinc@gmail.com>
Subject: Your S/C No. 432

Dear Jones,

We have been informed by our agents in Beijing that 200 kids toys under the above S/C by S.S. "Great Wall" arrived at Port Amsterdam on July 8th. Much to our regret, about 20% of the packages were seriously damaged with contents shattered to pieces and the outer bands broken.

We immediately invited qualified surveyors to the spot to look into the case, and their findings show that this was due to poor packing. A detailed survey report will be dispatched to you subsequent to their further study of individual case.

In accordance with the stipulations of the above Sales Confirmation, we think the kids toys should have been packed in strong seaworthy wooden cases suitable for long distance ocean voyages. We are obliged to hold that you are responsible for the damage and claim on you for the compensation for the loss thus incurred.

Meanwhile our buyers are urging us to settle the case immediately. Therefore, we would like you to inform us of what you decide to do regarding our losses.

We are awaiting your prompt reply.

Yours faithfully,

David

11.2.2 Basic Writing Structures of Letters Concerning Dealing with Complaints or Claims

Every complaint or claim, no matter how trivial it seems, is important to the person who makes it. It, therefore, requires a prompt answer or acknowledgment. The answer should be factual, courteous and fair. When replying to complaints, plan your letter as follows:

1. Begin with a reference to the date of the original letter of complaint and to the purpose of your letter;

2. Review the complaint and the action you are taking;

3. Explain in detail about the actions being or not being done;

4. If you deny the request, try to offer some partial or substitute compensation or offer some friendly advice;

5. Conclude the letter cordially, perhaps expressing the wish of future contact.

Letter 3　Seller's Reply to the Shortages

To: "J. Wong" <wondertoyscoltd@hotmail.com>
From: "David" <forevertradeinc@gmail.com>
Subject: Order No. 768197

Dear Mr. Wong,

Re: Order No. 768197

Please accept our apologies for the error made by our company in fulfilling your order No. 768197 dated May 17th, 2024.

You ordered 12,000 R/C toys, but our dispatch office sent 1,200 R/C toys. This was due to a typing error.

The remaining of 10,800 R/C toys were dispatched by express courier to your store this morning and will arrive by Monday, July 5th, 2024.

Since we value your business, we would like to offer you a 10% discount off for your next order with us.

We look forward to receiving your further orders and assure you that they will be fulfilled correctly.

Yours sincerely,
David Choi

Unit 11 Complaints and Adjustments

Letter 4 Seller's Reply to Complaint for Improper Packing: Refusal to the Claim

To: "David" <forevertradeinc@gmail.com>
From: "Jones" <curetoyscoltd@hotmail.com>
Subject: Reply to Your S/C No. 432

Dear David,

    We feel deeply sorry that the 200 kids toys under the S/C No. 432 by S.S. "Great Wall" arrived at Port Amsterdam on July 8 with 20% of the packages damaged as mentioned in your letter of October 11th, 2023.

    You may be aware that our kids toys have been sold in a number of markets abroad for quite a long time, and all our customers have been satisfied with our packing. Each shipment of our exports is strictly inspected by our shipping departments before loading, and each package is subject to a careful examination. So we think that the goods were in perfect condition when they were shipped, and individual packages were clearly marked with "Handle With Care", "Fragile" and other necessary indicative marks. The clean B/L supports these facts.

    After going into the matter carefully, we estimate that the damage might be due to rough handling in transportation or during loading and unloading. We consider it a matter for you to take up with the shipping company or the insurers who have covered you on the said consignment against Risk of Breakage. The responsibility should rest with either of the parties concerned. Consequently, we find no ground to compensate you for the loss.

Yours faithfully,
Jones

Useful Words & Expressions

I. Widely-used Terms

1. improper packing	包装不当	2. qualified surveyors	有资质的检验员
3. poor packing	不良包装	4. survey report	调查报告
5. express courier	快递	6. clean B/L	清洁提单
7. shipping company	船运公司	8. insurer	保险公司、承保人

185

II. Important Phrases

1. in a difficult position　　　　陷于困境
2. fulfill one's commitment　　　履行承诺
3. considerable inconvenience　　相当麻烦
4. make up the shortfall　　　　 补足短数
5. look into　　　　　　　　　　调查
6. long distance ocean voyages　 远洋航行
7. settle the case　　　　　　　 了结此案
8. dispatch office　　　　　　　 调度室
9. typing error　　　　　　　　 打字输入错误
10. 10% discount off　　　　　　10%的折扣(打九折)
11. shipping departments　　　　装运部
12. go into　　　　　　　　　　 细查
13. rough handling　　　　　　　粗暴搬运
14. take up with　　　　　　　　与……交涉
15. rest with　　　　　　　　　 在于
16. no ground　　　　　　　　　 没有理由

III. Purpose of Writing (Background Information)

1. The B/O toys you shipped per S.S. "Peace" on March 2nd arrived here yesterday.

2. We are, therefore, compelled to claim on you to compensate us for the loss, $1,000, which we have sustained by the damage to the goods.

3. **I am writing to inform you that** the goods we ordered from your company have not been supplied correctly.

4. **Please accept our apologies for** the error made by our company in fulfilling your order No. 768197 dated May 17th, 2024.

5. **We feel deeply sorry that** the 200 kids toys under the S/C No. 432 by S.S. "Great Wall" arrived at Port Amsterdam on July 8th with 20% of the packages damaged as mentioned in your letter of October 11th, 2023.

6. **We have been informed** by our agents in Beijing that 200 kids toys under the above S/C by S.S. "Great Wall" arrived at Port Amsterdam on July 8th.

7. **I am writing to** ask you to please make up the shortfall immediately and to ensure that such errors do not happen again.

IV. Letters of Complaints or Claims

Reasons for Complaints or Claims

1. On examination, nearly 20% of **the packages had been broken** and the toys were in pieces. It was obviously attributed to improper packing.

2. On May 17th, 2024 we placed an order with your firm for 12,000 R/C toys. The consignment arrived yesterday but it contained only 1,200 R/C toys.

On July 17th, 2024, we **placed an order** with your firm for 12,000 ultra super long-life batteries. The consignment arrived yesterday but it contained only 1,200 batteries.

3. **This error put our firm in a difficult position**, as we had to make some emergency purchases to fulfill our commitments to all our customers.

This caused us considerable inconvenience.

4. **Much to our regret**, about 20% of the packages were seriously damaged with contents shattered to pieces and the outer bands broken.

5. We immediately invited qualified surveyors to the spot to **look into the case**, and their findings show that this was **due to poor packing**.

6. **A detailed survey report will be dispatched to you** subsequent to their further study of individual case.

7. Firstly, I had difficulty in registering to attend the event. You set up an online registration facility, but I found the facility totally **unworkable**.

8. You sent us an invoice for $10,532, but did not deduct our usual 10% discount.

9. We have found 16 spelling errors and 2 mislabeled diagrams in the sample book.

10. Even after spending several hours trying to register in this way, the computer would not accept my application.

11. I am returning the invoice to you for correction.

12. This large number of errors is unacceptable to our customers, and we are unable to sell these books.

Suggestions for Improving the Situation/Solving the Problems

1. **We should like to take this opportunity to suggest that** special care be taken in your future deliveries.

2. Please make up the shortfall immediately and **ensure that** such errors will not be made again. Otherwise, we may have to look elsewhere for our supplies.

3. **In accordance with** the stipulations of the above Sales Confirmation, we think the kids toys should have been packed in strong seaworthy wooden cases suitable for long distance ocean

voyages.

4. **We are obliged to** hold you are responsible for the damage and claim on you for the compensation for the loss thus incurred.

5. Meanwhile our buyers are **urging us to settle the case immediately**. Therefore, **we would like you to** inform us of what you decide to do regarding our losses.

6. Could I ask you to look into these matters?

7. Please send us a corrected invoice for USD9,479.

8. I enclose a copy of the book with the errors highlighted. Please reprint the book and send it to us by next Friday.

9. **I'm afraid that** if these conditions are not met, we may be forced to take legal actions.

10. If the outstanding fees are not paid by Friday, August 2nd, 2024, you will incur a 10% late payment fee.

V. Reply to Letters of Complaints or Claims

Expressing Thanks / Making an Apology

1. **Please accept our apologies for the error** made by our company in fulfilling your order No. 768197 dated May 17th, 2024.

2. **We feel deeply sorry that...**

3. **Thank you for your letter of**… regarding/concerning/in connection with…

4. I refer to your letter of… about/relating to…

5. **Apology for the error or fault...**

6. **We must apologize for…**

We sincerely apologize for…

7. **I would like to apologize for** the error made by our company in... (verb+ing)

Giving Detailed Explanation of the Fault

1. You ordered 12,000 R/C toys, but our dispatch office sent 1,200 R/C toys. This was due to a typing error.

2. The remaining of 10,800 R/C toys were dispatched by express courier to your store this morning and will arrive by Monday, July 5th, 2024.

3. All our customers have been satisfied with our packing.

4. Each shipment of our exports is strictly inspected by our shipping departments before loading, and each package is subject to a careful examination.

5. So we think that the goods were in perfect condition when they were shipped, and

individual packages were clearly marked with "Handle With Care", "Fragile" and other necessary indicative marks. The clean B/L supports these facts.

6. After going into the matter carefully, we estimate that the damage might be due to rough handling in transportation or during loading and unloading.

7. The error was caused by…/was due to…

8. Apparently, the problem was the result of…/resulted from…

9. The cause of/reason for the mistake was…

Solutions/Proposals

Accepting the Complaint

1. Since we value your business, **we would like to offer you** a 10% discount off for your next order with us.

2. **We have modified/changed our...**

3. **We have implemented a system to...**

4. **To prevent re-occurrences** we have set up a verification procedure.

5. **We assure you that** this will not happen again.

6. **We are currently investigating the cause of...**

We will investigate the cause of...

7. As a gesture of our regret, **we are prepared to… / we are willing to… / we would like to…**

8. **To show our goodwill, we would like to** offer you a 5% discount on your next order with us.

9. **We have dispatched the new items** by express courier. They should arrive by Monday, July 29th, 2024.

Declining the Complaint

1. **We consider it a matter for you** to take up with the shipping company or the insurers who have covered you on the said consignment against Risk of Breakage.

2. **The responsibility should rest with** either of the parties concerned. Consequently, we find no ground to compensate you for the loss.

3. **While we can understand your frustration, ...**

4. **We understand** how disappointing it can be when your expectations are not met.

5. **I regret to inform you that…**

6. **I am afraid that…**

7. **Unfortunately, I must point out that…**

8. **This is because** the guarantee period has expired.

9. **This is due to the fact that** the guarantee period has expired.

10. If a third party (another person or organization) **is to blame**, direct the complainer to that party.

11. **We therefore suggest that you contact...**

VI. Expectations for Further Contact

1. **We hope** we can get a satisfactory answer within one week. We are waiting for your early reply.

2. **I look forward to hearing from you.**

I look forward to hearing from you shortly.

3. **We are awaiting** your prompt reply.

4. **We look forward to** receiving your further orders and assure you that they will be fulfilled correctly.

I look forward to receiving your explanation of these matters.

Exercises

I. Choose the best answer to complete each of the following sentences.

1. Your claim for the damage is to be _____ with the insurance company.

    A. met   B. filed   C. satisfied   D. compensated

2. Will you please let us know the details of any lines of goods which you think are _____ for your market.

    A. interesting   B. suitable   C. proper   D. desirable

3. They made a _____ on us for the damage.

    A. communication   B. discount   C. reference   D. claim

4. _____ your needs, please write to us with your specific inquires.

    A. Should these new products suit   B. Had these new products suited

    C. If these new products would suit   D. If these new products were to suit

5. It is important that your client ____ the relevant L/C not later than April 15th, 2024.

    A. must open   B. has to open   C. open   D. opens

6. The goods ____ shipped already if your L/C had arrived by the end of December.

    A. would be   B. must have been   C. had been   D. would have been

Unit 11 Complaints and Adjustments

7. The buyer suggested that the packing of this article _____ improved.

   A. be   B. was to be   C. would be   D. had to be

8. If we had a sample in hand, we _____ to negotiate business with our end-users now.

   A. would be able   B. should have

   C. had been able   D. should have been able

9. The goods under Contract No. 15408 left here _____.

   A. in a good condition   B. in good conditions

   C. in good condition   D. in the good condition

10. We have lodged a claim _____ ABC & Co. _____ the quality of the goods shipped _____ M.V. "Peace".

    A. against, for, by   B. with, for, under

    C. on, against, as per   D. to, for, per

11. As the goods are ready for shipment, we _____ your L/C to be opened immediately.

    A. hope   B. anticipate   C. await   D. expect

12. As arranged, we have effected insurance _____ the goods _____ 110% of the invoice value _____ all risks.

    A. of, at, with   B. for, in, against   C. on, for, against D. to, at over

II. Fill in the blanks with the appropriate words or expressions.

1. The buyers are complaining _____ the wrong goods _____ the sellers.

2. We are holding the goods of faulty good _____ your disposal.

3. As the damage occurred during transit, please direct your claim _____ the insurance company.

4. Our clients have claimed _____ us _____ delayed delivery of the goods.

5. We regret to say that we have to lodge our claim _____ the Arbitration Committee.

6. This delay is causing us serious inconvenience because we promise delivery _____ the strength of your assurance.

7. The shipment is short-invoiced _____ RMB￥8,600 and we have drawn a draft on you _____ the balance.

8. Please fax your confirmation on receipt of our remittance for US$5,000 in settlement _____ the claim.

III. Give the English/Chinese equivalents of the following expressions.

1. 赔偿，补偿 _____   2. 处理索赔理赔_____

3. 检验报告 ＿＿＿＿＿＿＿＿＿＿

4. 仲裁 ＿＿＿＿＿＿＿＿＿＿

5. 申诉 ＿＿＿＿＿＿＿＿＿＿

6. authorized surveyor ＿＿＿＿＿

7. poor packing ＿＿＿＿＿＿＿

8. inferior quality ＿＿＿＿＿＿

9. short-delivered ＿＿＿＿＿＿

10. China Commodity Inspection Bureau ＿＿＿＿＿＿＿＿＿＿

IV. Translate the following sentences into English/Chinese.

1. 非常遗憾地通知你方，发运给我方的货物没有达到规定的标准。

2. 我方由贵方6月6号来函获悉，由我方承运的木箱包装的货物中发现有几件破损，我方对此感到遗憾。

3. 关于你方产品品质低劣的问题，我方要求你方赔偿一万美元。

4. 从你方5月8日的来函中获知我方发错了玩具，对此我方深感抱歉。

5. 我方对此事带来的不便深表歉意，并保证将采取一切措施避免此类差错再次发生。

6. We are unable to accept the shipment which we received from you today, as they had been completely smashed when they reached us.

7. A claim has been filed on you for shortage of kids shoes shipped on board S.S. "Victory" which arrived here on May 24th.

8. We regret that your claim on shortage cannot be accepted.

9. The wrong pieces may be returned per next available steamer for our account, but it is preferable if you dispose of them in your market.

10. As our shipping documents can confirm that the goods were in perfect condition when they left here, that evidently shows they were damaged in transportation.

V. Translate the following letters into English/Chinese.

Letter 1

敬启者：

事由：投诉货物质量问题

12月7日订购的900打第222号丝巾订单现已运抵本公司。经查验后本公司很失望地发现货物的质量与您之前寄来的样品不一致。

该批货物颜色与样本颜色相差甚远，部分质量极低劣，令人怀疑订购过程可能出现错误。由于货物颜色与本公司要求不符，因此我公司要求退货，并换回订单要求之货物。

本公司诚意希望能友好地解决该问题。如贵公司接受上述安排，本公司准备待贵公司确能供应合格货物起计算交货日期。

盼早复。

谨上

进口部经理　露西·王

Letter 2　Complaint of Wrong Goods Delivery

Dear Sirs,

　　We are writing to complain about the shipment of our Order No. SR112 for 3,000 dozen men's sports shoes received this morning. These were ordered on July 20th, 2023 and confirmed by fax on August 8th(enclosed copy). However, upon opening the boxes, we found that they contained 3,000 dozen women's garden shoes, and we can only presume that a mistake was made and the contents were for another order.

　　As our clients are badly in need of the sports shoes we ordered, we cannot but ask you to arrange for the dispatch of replacement at once. Even so, delay shipment is deemed to occur, and you should pay us USD 5,000 as liquidated damages.

　　With regard to the mis-dispatched cargoes, please instruct us how to deal with them immediately, otherwise we will return them to you at your cost.

　　We await your early reply.

Yours Sincerely,

Tony Smith

VI. Writing.

1. Write a letter of claim for inferior quality based on the following particulars:

(1) 929 号订单项下的 100 箱羊毛毯已收到；

(2) 检验报告表明货物未达到样品的标准，质量低劣无法适合此地市需求；

(3) 要求退回货物，并提出索赔发票金额和检验费共计……；

(4) 希望早日解决索赔。

2. Write a letter of reply to Letter 2 in exercise V about the mis-dispatched cargoes, and the letter can include the following points:

(1) 确认收到来信，遗憾客户投诉货物发错了。

(2) 经调查，错发货物系库存数据失误造成，深表遗憾。

(3) 解决如下：①立即重新发货；②同意支付延迟交货违约金，但希望对方能少收些；③错发的货物不要退回，而是希望对方请求客户购买，同意给予价格优惠。

(4) 希望早日得到回复。

微课视频

扫一扫，获取本课相关微课视频。

11.1.1　Case Study.mp4

11.1.2　Relevant Information.mp4

11.1.3　Writing Skills.mp4

11.2.1　Letter 1 Buyer's Claim for Short Weight.mp4

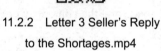
11.2.2　Letter 3 Seller's Reply to the Shortages.mp4

Bibliography

[1] 鲍文，孙志农，柯应根. 商务英语写作[M]. 合肥：安徽大学出版社，2020.
[2] 陈杰，刘元直. 商务英语写作精讲[M]. 北京：清华大学出版社，2017.
[3] 董晓波. 国际贸易英语函电[M]. 2 版. 北京：清华大学出版社、北京交通大学出版社，2017.
[4] 房玉靖，马国志. 商务英语写作[M]. 2 版. 北京：清华大学出版社，2021.
[5] 洪菁，陈淑霞. 国际商务英语函电[M]. 4 版. 北京：对外经济贸易大学出版社，2020.
[6] 刘媛. 外贸英语函电[M]. 2 版. 北京：清华大学出版社，2021.
[7] 刘怡，丁言仁. 商务英语写作教程[M]. 上海：上海外语教育出版社，2016.
[8] 王艳艳. 商务沟通与函电[M]. 上海：华东师范大学出版社，2020.
[9] 滕美荣，许楠. 外贸英语函电[M]. 5 版. 北京：首都经济贸易大学出版社，2017.
[10] 吴雯. 国际商务英语函电[M]. 4 版. 北京：北京大学出版社，2020.
[11] 杨伶俐. 外贸英语函电[M]. 3 版. 北京：对外经济贸易大学出版社，2021.
[12] 易露霞，刘洁，尤彧聪. 外贸英语函电[M]. 4 版. 北京：清华大学出版社，2020.
[13] 尹小莹，张欣. 外贸英语函电[M]. 6 版. 西安：西安交通大学出版社，2019.
[14] Shirley Taylor. 商务英语写作实例精解[M]. 7 版. 卢艳春，白荣梅，译. 北京：外语教学与研究出版社，2014.